FACTS AT YOUR FINGERTIPS

ANCIENT
EGYPT

WAYLAND

This edition published in 2009 by Wayland (a division of Hachette Children's Books)

Wayland
Hachette Children's Books
338 Euston Road
London NW1 3BH

Wayland Australia
Level 17/207 Kent Street
Sydney NSW 2000

© 2009 The Brown Reference Group Ltd

The Brown Reference Group Ltd
First Floor
9–17 St Albans Place
London N1 0NX
www.brownreference.com

ISBN 978-07502-6079-4

Printed in the United States of America.

Wayland is a division of Hachette Children's Books, an Hachette UK Company.
www.hachette.co.uk

10 9 8 7 6 5 4 3 2 1

Editorial Director: Lindsey Lowe
Managing Editor: Tim Cooke
Design Manager: David Poole
Designer: Sarah Williams
Picture Manager: Sophie Mortimer
Picture Researcher: Sean Hannaway
Text Editor: Anita Dalal
Indexer: Indexing Specialists (UK) Ltd

CONTENTS

A Lasting Civilisation

This book is about ancient Egypt, one of the great civilisations of the past. The ancient Greeks saw Egypt as the source of all wisdom. Roman emperors travelled to Egypt to marvel at monuments such as the pyramids. Egyptian statues and obelisks were sent to decorate Rome. The worship of Egyptian gods and goddesses such as Isis and Osiris spread through the Roman Empire as far as Britain.

Extensive Ruins

The modern fascination with Egypt began in the late 18th century. Since then, a huge number of ancient towns, temples and tombs have been excavated. No country in the world has so many impressive ancient remains as Egypt does. In the Nile Valley the past seems very close. The people who lived there thousands of years ago have left us a wonderful legacy of art, architecture and literature.

Structure of the Book

Ancient Egypt is divided into two main sections. The first tells the story of Egypt from the union of the country in about 3100 BCE to the coming of the Romans almost 3,000 years later. Archaeologists break up the great span of Egyptian history into a series of periods and 'kingdoms'.

The Predynastic Period was the era before Egypt was united under a single ruler. From the Early Dynastic Period, Egypt was ruled by dynasties of kings. A dynasty was a sequence of rulers, usually related by blood or marriage. The eras known as kingdoms were times when Egypt was strong and united. The 'intermediate periods' between the kingdoms were times when the country was weak and divided. The last dynasties of native Egyptian kings ruled during the Late Period, at the end of Egypt's history as an independent nation. In the Greco-Roman Period, Egypt was first under Greek and then under Roman rule.

Egyptian History

The first part of the book tells the history of ancient Egypt. For each kingdom or period, you will find a panel listing the dynasties that ruled during the time. The names and dates of the most important rulers in each dynasty are also given. The exact spelling and pronunciation of most ancient Egyptian names is uncertain because vowels were not written in full. Ideas about how the names should be written out in English have changed as our knowledge of ancient languages has grown. The name that used to be spelled Tutankhamen is now usually written as Tutankhamun or Tutankhamon, for example. It means 'Living Image of the god Amon'.

The maps highlight the location of places or sites that were important in each period or kingdom, or where archaeological finds have been made..

Journey Down the Nile

The second part of this book, beginning on pages 32–33, takes you on a journey down the Nile. The journey starts in Lower Nubia, a country to the south of Egypt, and ends at the Mediterranean coast. There is a map for each region. These are maps of modern Egypt but they mark all the important ancient sites and structures that survive. For most sites a modern Arabic name and at least one ancient name are given. Some of these ancient names are Egyptian. Others date to the time when the Greeks ruled Egypt. Beside the site names are symbols to show you what kind of ancient remains have been found there.

Abbreviations used in this book

BCE = Before Common Era (also known as BC).

CE = Common Era (also known as AD).

c. = circa (about).

in = inch; ft = foot; yd = yard; mi = mile.

cm = centimetre; m = metre; km = kilometre.

This relief on the wall of a temple at Karnak, Luxor, shows the 18th-Dynasty pharaoh Amenhotep IV. When he came to the throne in 1353 BCE, the pharaoh took the name Akenhaten and tried to get the Egyptians to follow a new religion dedicated to the sun god, Aten. After he died, however, the country returned to its older forms of worship.

TIMELINES

EGYPTIAN HISTORY

Predynastic
Badarian/Tasian culture, Nile valley c.4500–4000.
Merimda cultures, Delta c.4800–4100.
Faiyum culture c.5400–4400.

Predynastic
Naqada I, Nile valley c.4000–3500.
Naqada II–III, Nile valley c.3500–3100.
Invention of writing.

Foundation of Egyptian state c.3100.
Trade with Mesopotamia.

Early Dynastic Period c.2920–2575.
1st–3rd Dynasties.
First mining expeditions to Sinai.

Old Kingdom c.2575–2134.
4th–6th Dynasties.
Raids on Libya, Palestine and Lower Nubia. Trade with Upper Nubia.

First Intermediate Period c.2134–2040
7th–11th Dynasties.
Rival dynasties and civil wars.

Hunters from stone palette, c.3000 BCE

Tomb stela of King Wadj from Abydos, c.2980 BCE

Statue of King Khephren from Giza, c.2495 BCE

ARCHITECTURE AND TOMBS

Reed huts.

Graves under hut floors at Merimda Beni Salama.

Reed shrines.

First buildings in mud-brick.

Walled town and brick-lined tombs at Hierakonpolis.

Mud-brick 'funerary palaces' at Abydos.

Mud-brick mastaba tombs at Saqqara.

First stone buildings.

Massive stone pyramids and stone mastaba tombs at Giza, Saqqara and Abusir.

Stone sun temples and obelisks at Abu Ghurab and Abusir.

Painted terra-cotta figurine of a dancer, c.4000 BCE

Step pyramids at Saqqara.

Painting of geese from a tomb at Maidum, c.2560 BCE

Step Pyramid of King Djoser at Saqqara, c.2560 BCE

ART AND CRAFTS

Fine pottery vessels, clay figurines, objects carved from ivory.

Painted pottery, stone palettes and vessels, terra-cotta and ivory figurines.

First wall paintings and stone statuettes.

Large stone statues.

First reliefs in wood and stone.

First stone stelae.

Gold jewellery.

Faience figurines.

Painted tomb reliefs of daily life.

Royal statues in hard stones or in copper.

Private statues in stone or wood.

Furniture in wood and decorated sheet gold.

...le Kingdom c.2040–1640.
...13th Dynasties.
...on of Egypt under Theban
...asty.
... with Syria and Palestine.
...ation of Lower Nubia.

**...d Intermediate Period
...640–1532.**
...17th Dynasties.
...ation of Delta by Hyksos
...n Syria/Palestine.
...a culture occupies Lower
...ia. War between the
Hyksos and
Theban
kings.

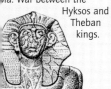
...e of King Senwosret III from
...l-Bahri, c.1850 BCE

**Early New Kingdom
1550–1307.**
17th–18th Dynasties.
Egypt reunited under Theban
dynasty.
Conquest of Lower and Upper
Nubia.
Rise of Egyptian empire in
Syria and Palestine.

Gold mask from the mummy of
King Tutankhamon, c.1325 BCE

**Late New Kingdom
c.1307–1196.**
19th–20th Dynasties. Wars
against the Hittites in Syria.
Depopulation of Lower Nubia.
Wars against the Sea Peoples.
Gradual loss of Near Eastern
empire.

Colossal statue at the Great
Temple of Abu Simbel, c.1270 BCE

**Third Intermediate Period
c.1070–712.**
21st–25th Dynasties.
Egypt divided.
Kings ruling Delta and High
Priests ruling Thebes.
Rise of Nubian Kingdom of
Napata.
Civil wars among petty rulers.

Late Period 712–332.
25th–30th Dynasties
Egypt reunited by Nubian kings.
Conquest of Egypt by the
Assyrians and by the Persians.
Periods of native rule between
conquests.

Kneeling
Egyptian from
statue base
of a Persian king,
c.500 BCE

**Greco-Roman Period
332 BCE–395 CE**
Greek rule 332–30 BCE
Egypt ruled by Ptolemies.
Many Greek immigrants. Some
Egyptian rebellions.
Roman rule 30 BCE–395 CE
Egypt becomes part of the
Roman Empire.
Most of Nubia ruled by Kings
of Meroe.

Head of a priest in green
schist, c.75 BCE

...mortuary temple of
...ntuhotep III at Deir
...ahri.
...rick pyramids in Middle
...t and at Dahshur.
...ut tombs in Middle Egypt.
...in Nubia.

...en figurine
...ervant from
...ban tomb,
...0 BCE

Terraced temple of Hatshepsut
at Deir el-Bahri.
Rock-cut royal tombs in the
Valley of the Kings.
Temples of Amon at Karnak
and Luxor.
Palaces and Aten temples at
el-Amarna.

Relief from a vizier's tomb
at Thebes, c.1360 BCE

Mortuary temples of Ramesses
II (The Ramesseum) and
Ramesses III (Medinet Habu)
at Thebes.
Great Hypostyle Hall at
Karnak, Ramesses II.
Great Temple of Abu Simbel
and other rock-cut and
freestanding temples in
Nubia.

Relief of a blind harpist from
a Saqqara tomb, c.1300 BCE

Temple of Amon at Tanis with
underground royal tombs.
Large tombs with mud-brick
pylons at Thebes.
Shaft tombs at Saqqara.
Granite temple of Isis at Behbeit
el-Hagar.

Inlaid bronze figure of a
high priestess, c.850 BCE

Great Egyptian-style temples at
Philae, Kom Ombo, Edfu,
Esna and Dendara.
Greco-Egyptian style 'funerary
houses' at Tuna el-Gebel.
Underground galleries of
tombs at Alexandria.

Facade of the temple of Hathor
at Dendara, c.34 CE

...portrait sculpture.
...paintings of daily life.
...ed wooden models of
...y life.
...ewellery in gold and
...iprecious stones.

Temple reliefs with royal and
religious scenes.
Monumental sculpture.
Tomb paintings and painted
reliefs of daily life.
Decorated pottery and faience
vessels.

Colossal stone statues.
Temple reliefs with battle
and hunting scenes.
Illustrated 'Books of the Dead'.
Tomb paintings of religious
scenes.

Faience bowls and chalices.
Bronze figurines.
Private sculpture in hard stones.
Decorated cartonnage coffins
and stone sarcophagi.

Portrait sculpture in hard
stones.
Temple reliefs of religious
scenes.
Faience and terra-cotta
figurines.
Painted 'mummy portraits'.

EGYPT, GIFT OF THE NILE

Ancient Egyptian civilisation was shaped by its geographical location within north-eastern Africa. It grew up in the narrow Nile Valley, which was isolated on both sides by desert. Nearby West Asia was where agriculture first began. The ancient Egyptians developed highly efficient ways of farming. They were able to grow enough food to support Egypt's population throughout most of its history. The annual crops depended on the regular flooding of the river. Without the Nile, ancient Egypt would not have come into being more than 5,000 years ago. The ancient Greek historian Herodotus called Egypt 'the gift of the Nile'.

A Fertile Corridor

About 12,000 years ago, most of North Africa was covered by grassland (savanna) where animals grazed. Over time, the climate became drier and the savannah turned into desert. The world's longest river – the Nile – flowed through the desert. Even though there was virtually no rainfall in the valley itself, the river's waters supported rich vegetation growing in a narrow strip along its banks.

The Nile valley is a long, narrow corridor that varies in width from 19 kilometres (12 mi) wide to as little as 1.6 kilometres (1 mi) wide. Before it joins the Mediterranean Sea, the Nile splits into lots of small rivers that make up a delta. The delta is 200 kilometres (125 mi) wide.

The Black Land

The ancient Egyptians called their country the Black Land because the rich soil of the Nile Valley was a black colour. Over time, the climate changed the valley from a swamp and only the Delta kept large areas of marshland.

Every summer the rains far to the south, where the Nile has its source, raised the level of the river in Egypt. The Blue Nile rises in the Ethiopian Highlands. The White Nile rises south of Lake Victoria in central Africa and drains water from a large area of southern Sudan.

SYRIA
Qurnet el-Sawda 3083
EBANON
eirut Damascus
Syrian Desert
AEL
em Amman
JORDAN
Gebel Musa (Mt Sinai) 2287
Euphrates
MESOPOTAMIA
Tigris
Baghdad
IRAQ
ZAGROS MOUNTAINS
IRAN
Kuwait
KUWAIT
PERSIAN GULF
BAHRAIN
Manama
QATAR
Doha
NAFUD
SAUDI ARABIA
Riyadh
U.A.E
ARABIAN PENINSULA
RUB AL-KHALI
ert
Red Sea
ract
Cataract
Atbara
ERITREA
Asmara
PUNT
Dahlak Archipelago
San'a YEMEN
Hadur Shuaayb 3760
HADRAMAWT
NA
Ras Dashan 4620
Danakil Plain
Bab el-Mandeb
Gulf of Aden
DJIBOUTI
Djibouti
Lake Tana
ETHIOPIAN HIGHLANDS
Blue Nile
ETHIOPIA
Addis Ababa
SOMALIA
Ogaden
Batu 4307
Shebele
Lake Turkana
Mogadishu
INDIAN OCEAN
KENYA
Juba

The geography of Egypt today. The Nile is fed by the Blue and the White Nile. Its ultimate source is Lake Victoria, which is located in the south of Uganda.

The Inundation

Within what is now Egypt, the Nile regularly overflowed its banks. It flooded the low-lying fields on either side for about two months each year. The area covered in water was called the flood plain and the event was known as the inundation. When the waters went down, they left a layer of fertile mud. This silt was full of nutrients that made it perfect for growing crops. The level of flooding was crucial, however. Too much and villages might flood; too little and not enough crops would be able to be grown. The ancient Egyptians built 'nilometers' along the river. These structures enabled the Egyptians to measure the height of the river and therefore to be able to predict the seasonal flooding.

The Red Land

Deserts lie to the east and west of the Nile valley. The Egyptians called this the Red Land. To the west, the desert stretched into the huge Sahara. There are few settlements, apart from small areas of fertile land around oases, where water carried in underground layers of rock called aquifers rises to the surface. To the east, the desert rose to a range of mountains, which were cut through by wadis (dry river beds). These river beds were dry for most of the year, although they filled up with water after heavy rains. Both empty and full, the wadis were important trade routes across the desert and mountains to the coast of the Red Sea.

Natural Protection

The Nile is difficult to sail in the south of Egypt because of a series of rapids, which are known as cataracts. To the north, the marshes of the delta provided natural protection against people arriving from the Mediterranean. These natural barriers, together with the deserts to the east and west, made Egypt a difficult country to invade. They also isolated Egypt from its neighbours, helping to explain how Egypt's unique culture endured for so long.

THE LAND OF GOLD

Ancient Egyptian civilisation depended on a rich supply of natural resources. Many of them were imported from abroad by traders, but Egypt also possessed many resources of its own. Limestone, sandstone and granite for building temples and tombs came from the desert hills on the edge of the Nile Valley. Rarer stones, such as alabaster, were used for making vases and statues.

The Egyptian deserts also contained mines that extracted semi-precious stones and precious metals, especially gold. One foreign king wrote that in Egypt gold was as common as dust!

The Nile – A Precious Resource

The most precious resource in ancient Egypt was water. Almost no rain falls across Egypt, so the annual flooding of the Nile was vital for growing crops such as corn and barley. Another crop was flax, which was used to make linen for clothes. The finest ancient Egyptian linen was spun so finely you could see right through it.

People dug irrigation channels to carry water far from the Nile to gardens and orchards. Vegetables such as lettuce, onions, peas and lentils were grown, along with fruits such as figs and pomegranates.

The Nile also gave Egyptians their homes. Bricks were made from wet clay from the river bank and left in the sun to dry. All Egyptian houses were made from these mud bricks.

The Delta was the only part of Egypt where enough grass grew to feed large herds of cattle. The marshes were rich in bird, fish and plant life. The Egyptians fished with nets or spears and used boomerangs to hunt birds. Lotus flowers were made into perfume and reeds were made into boats and matting. The stems of papyrus plants were made into a sort of paper, which became one of Egypt's chief exports.

A seated nomarch (governor) oversees the cattle census. Cattle are driven past a kiosk to be counted and recorded by the scribes. The owners are then told how much tax they have to pay.

Main exports of ancient Egypt

Gold – Bags of gold dust or solid gold made into large rings.

Grain – Corn and any extra grain after a good harvest.

Papyrus – Made into scrolls and ready to write on.

Linens – Made from flax, the best quality was Royal Linen.

Main imports of ancient Egypt

Timber – Including cedar from Lebanon, used for shipbuilding, furniture and funeral coffins.

Bronze (copper/tin alloy) – Imported as ingots (metal bars) and used to make weapons, vessels and mirrors.

Iron – Imported after the 1st millennium BCE.

Ivory – From Africa for use in carvings and inlays.

Lapis Lazuli – Semi-precious stone from Afghanistan, used to make jewellery.

Incense – Imported from Punt (possibly present-day Eritrea) and the Yemen. Used for burning during religious rituals.

Oil – Used both for cooking and body oil.

Myrrh – Imported from Punt and Yemen and used to perfume the inside of mummies.

Exotic Animals – African animals such as monkeys, cheetahs, baboons and serval cats..

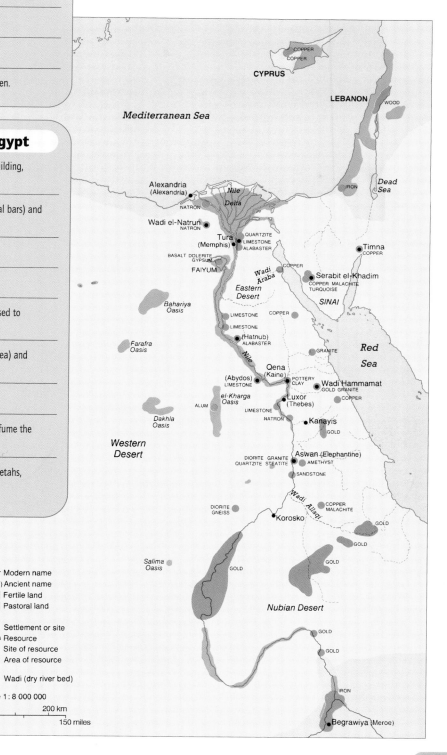

This map shows the very limited area of ancient Egypt that could be used for agriculture. The area of fertile land, particularly within the Delta, varied from season to season, year to year. Also marked are ancient mineral workings on the edges of the Nile valley and in the deserts. The turquoise mines of Sinai were highly prized by the Egyptians. The wadis (dry river beds) were used as trade routes.

Luxor Modern name
(Meroe) Ancient name
▢ Fertile land
▢ Pastoral land

● Settlement or site
NATRON Resource
● Site of resource
▢ Area of resource

---- Wadi (dry river bed)

Scale 1 : 8 000 000
0   200 km
0   150 miles

THE TWO KINGDOMS

Ancient Egypt was divided into two regions, known respectively as Upper and Lower Egypt. Upper Egypt was the narrow Nile valley. Lower Egypt was the north of the country, including the Delta region. The two lands were originally separate kingdoms, but were united under one ruler in about 3100 BCE. The rulers of the new kingdom were known as the Lords of the Two Lands. The location of the capital moved as families from different parts of Egypt came to the throne. Several of the capital cities were located near the border of Upper and Lower Egypt. This area was sometimes known as Middle Egypt.

Administrative Centres

For most of the long history of ancient Egypt, its population was probably no more than four million people. For the purposes of government, Upper and Lower Egypt were divided into districts called nomes. Each nome had its own administrative centre. These centres were probably quite small. Most Egyptians lived on farms or in small villages. Each village had a headman and each nome had its own governor, known as a nomarch.

The nomarchs ruled their districts on behalf of the kings. The nomarch's duties included maintaining the region's dykes and irrigation channels. This was a very important job because water was so precious. The nomarch also made sure that the grain was stored so that the local people could be fed during times of famine.

The First Civil Servants

Whichever city was the capital, it was home to a large number of officials who worked for the central government. The most important official was the vizier. He was in charge of public works, such as the building of monuments, and justice. At different times, there were two viziers, one for Upper and one for Lower Egypt.

The vizier was also responsible for collecting taxes. Until Egypt came under Greek control in

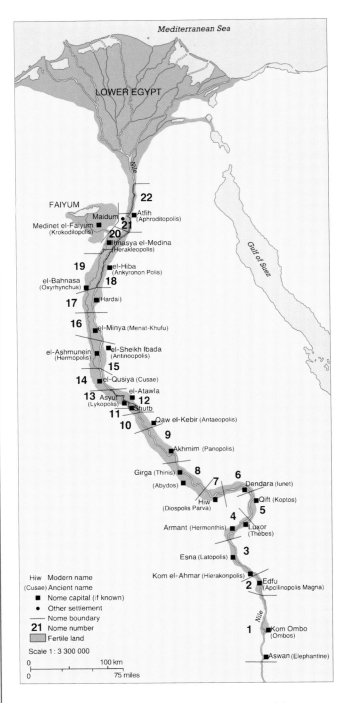

ABOVE: The nomes (districts) of Upper Egypt. The boundaries of the 22 nomes are based on a Middle Kingdom list. Some nomes had more than one capital during their history; in others the site of the capital is uncertain.

RIGHT: Lower Egypt was divided into 20 nomes. This map is based on nome lists in temples of the Greek and Roman (Greco-Roman) periods. Nome boundaries in the Delta were formed by the branches of the Nile.

Upper Egypt

1		9		17	
2		10		18	
3		11		19	
4		12		20	
5		13		21	
6		14		22	
7		15			
8		16			

Lower Egypt

1		8		15	
2		9		16	
3		10		17	
4		11		18	
5		12		19	
6		13		20	
7		14			

Each district, or nome, had a symbol. These symbols, or ensigns, were often derived from the form of a local god or goddess. In temple reliefs (carved scenes) the symbols are worn on the heads of figures that represent the nomes.

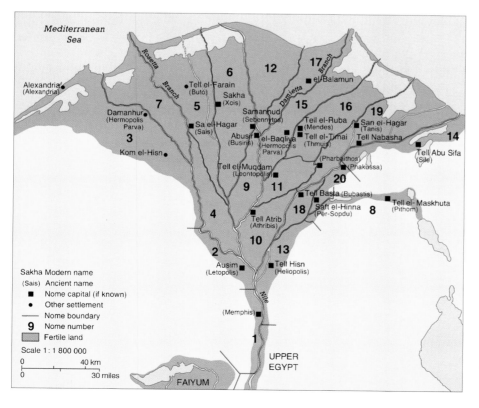

Sakha Modern name
(Sais) Ancient name
■ Nome capital (if known)
● Other settlement
— Nome boundary
9 Nome number
▨ Fertile land
Scale 1 : 1 800 000
0 — 40 km
0 — 30 miles

332 BCE, it did not have coins. Instead, taxes were paid with valuable goods, such as grain or cattle. All land ownership was registered and every two years all the cattle in Egypt were counted for the register.

Officials who worked in the vizier's office had to be good at lots of different jobs. One official noted in an inscription that during his career he was an inspector of pyramids, a judge and a tax collector. He also led an army, and oversaw the digging of canals and the quarrying of stone for pyramid building. He later became the governor of southern Egypt. Successful officials were well rewarded with luxury goods and country estates.

The very earliest Egyptians were nomads who hunted the wild animals that lived on the savanna while also herding their own domesticated animals. Over time, possibly because of the changing climate that made the savanna drier, people moved down into the Nile Valley. They began to settle in small communities along the river and raised crops for food. We know very little about these early people and how they lived, but we do know that there were different groups who followed different ways of life.

Predynastic Middle and Lower Egypt

In around 5400 BCE, one group of nomads settled in the region of the Faiyum, a large lake in the middle of Egypt. This community grew some crops, but its main source of food came from fishing in the lake. From other ancient sites excavated in Lower Egypt, archaeologists have learned that other groups of settlers grew corn, hunted desert animals and fished in the Nile.

At the oldest of the northern sites, Merimda Beni Salama in the western delta, people lived in clusters of huts made from reeds. They used stone tools, made simple clay pots and spun cloth into textiles for their clothes. At a later site near the southern end of the delta, Ma'adi,

there is evidence that people practiced growing crops, herding animals and metal working.

Predynastic Upper Egypt

In the south, the Badarian/Tasian culture spread along the Nile valley. These people lived in small villages scattered over the flood plain. They left many traces of their lives in the articles that they buried with their dead in cemeteries on the edge of the valley, where it met the desert. The grave goods were precious items for the dead, suggesting that the people practiced a religion that believed in an afterlife. They included decorated pots, bead necklaces, linen clothing and clay figures of people and animals, as well as amulets, ivory spoons and combs.

The Naqada Cultures

The Naqada I (or Amratian) culture was descended from the Badarian/Tasian people. The people were skilled stone workers who used flint to make rippled knives and arrowheads and made clubs from harder stones. The weapons were used for hunting desert animals, which were an important food source. Metal was still a rare material.

The Naqada II (or Gerzean) people were more technologically advanced than their ancestors. They lived in large tribal communities

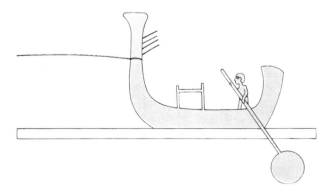

River traffic and trade on the Nile became important before dynastic times in Egypt. This Predynastic boat was made from papyrus reeds woven together. It had a tall prow and stern and was steered with a single large oar.

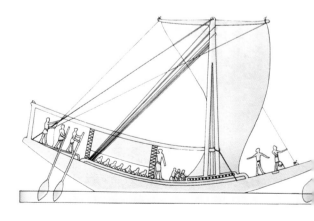

By the time of the Old Kingdom, boats had evolved into wooden craft with distinctively shaped hulls and double-footed masts that supported sails that were taller than they were wide.

that seem to have fought frequently among each other. Some of their burial goods suggest that the ruling classes of this period had grown very wealthy. The goods included jewellery made from gold and lapis lazuli, elaborate slate palettes used to grind eye makeup, as well as beautiful ivory combs and knife handles.

Trade in the Predynastic Period

By the Naqada III period a series of chieftains, who called themselves kings, had emerged to rule all of Upper Egypt. These kings are sometimes known as Dynasty 0, to suggest that they were very similar to the first dynasty to rule all of Egypt. Some objects from the period are decorated with designs from Mesopotamia (modern-day Iraq).

Archaeologists used to think that the rapid changes that took place in ancient Egypt at the end of the Predynastic Period must have been the result of the influence of newcomers. They suggested that foreigners may have invaded from the east and taken power, bringing Mesopotamian ideas with them. There is, however, no physical evidence of an invasion, although the different goods found in tombs proves the Egyptians were trading goods and ideas with people to the east.

About this time, the Upper Egyptians probably started to mine and export gold. The important early town of Ombos, near Naqada, was close to a major gold mining area.

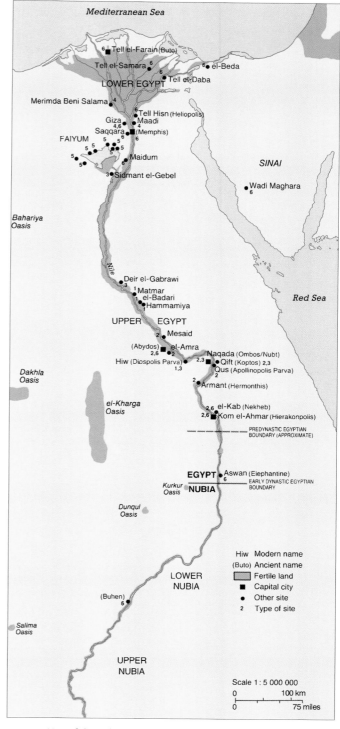

Most of the major Predynastic sites were on the margins of the desert. By Early Dynastic times many of these sites had been abandoned and new settlements were founded on the Nile's flood plain. The key numbers on the map relate to the numbers in the box (left).

MAJOR PREDYNASTIC AND EARLY DYNASTIC SITES

Dates for Predynastic cultures are uncertain. The development of Upper and Lower Egypt cannot easily be related. The numbers in the list refer to the numbers on the map.

1. **Badarian/Tasian** – c.4500–4000 BCE
2. **Naqada I** – c.4000–3500 BCE
3. **Naqada II** – c.3500–3000 BCE
4. **Lower Egypt** – c.4800–3000 BCE
5. **Faiyum** – c.5400–4400 BCE
6. **Naqada III and early Dynasties** – c.3200–2575 BCE

THE FIRST PYRAMIDS

Ancient Egyptian legend recorded that Upper and Lower Egypt were first united by a king named Menes. According to the story, Menes was a king of Upper Egypt who conquered Lower Egypt and founded a new capital at Memphis. The real identity of Menes remains a mystery. Two early kings have both been identified as the legendary founder. Their names, Narmer and Aha, are found on their tombs in the city of Abydos. Events that actually took place during the reigns of both of these kings may have added to the legend of Menes and the founding of the First Dynasty.

Early Dynastic Egypt

From the founding of the First Dynasty, historians are able to trace Egyptian history more closely, because the Egyptians themselves increasingly began to record events. They used a kind of picture writing known as hieroglyphics, which was only used in Egypt and was probably the oldest form of writing in the world.

During the First Dynasty, towns appeared alongside the traditional small villages, and homes made from mud bricks replaced reed huts. Tombs for important officials were made from mud bricks at Saqqara, the cemetery for the town of Memphis. The brick tombs (mastaba) were large rectangular flat-topped structures, which contained storerooms full of goods close to the burial chamber. Stone stelae, which were pillars carved with inscriptions, were placed next to the wall of one of the mastaba tombs at the spot where offerings were made to the dead. It was not unusual for some of the servants of a dead king to be killed and buried near his body so that their spirits could continue to serve him in the next life.

Khasekhemwy

Despite the development of the hieroglyphs, little is known about the history of Early Dynastic Egypt. It seems likely that during the Second Dynasty there was a civil war between two kings named Peribsen and Khasekhemwy. The kings were followers of two rival gods, Set and Horus. When

SELECTED KINGS OF THE EARLY DYNASTIC PERIOD 3100–2575 BCE	
1st Dynasty 3100–2770	Ninetjer
Narmer (=Aha? Menes?)	Peribsen
Djer	Khasekhemwy
Djet	
Den	**3rd Dynasty 2649–2575**
Semerkhet	Nebka 2649–2630
	Djoser 2630–2611
2nd Dynasty 2770–2649	Sekhemkhet 2611–2603
Hetepsekhemwy	Khaba 2603–2599
Reneb	Huni 2599–2575

Khasekhemwy emerged as the victor, he included the names of both the gods in writing with his name. This was possibly a peace gesture towards his defeated rival and his followers.

Khasekhemwy is the earliest Egyptian king for whom a stone statue survives. Unfortunately, grave robbers have robbed all the royal tombs of the First and Second Dynasties. Among the few objects to escape the robbers are treasures that reveal a high degree of skill. In the tomb of King Djer at Abydos, archaeologists found four bracelets made of gold, lapis lazuli and turquoise. The bracelets were still attached to an arm torn from a mummy in ancient times by tomb robbers.

Imhotep and the Step Pyramid

The reign of King Djoser from 2630 to 2611 BCE, during the Third Dynasty, was remembered by later ancient Egyptians as a golden age. One of Djoser's most important government officials was a man named Imhotep. Modern scholars often identify Imhotep as the first known individual from history who deserves the description of 'genius'. Imhotep is thought to have written books about medicine and was later worshipped by the Egyptians as a god of healing.

Later Egyptians also credited Imhotep with inventing stone architecture using mud bricks. That is highly unlikely, but Imhotep may deserve credit for designing Egypt's first pyramid – the Step Pyramid at Saqqara – for King Djoser.

Imhotep's name has been found inside the Step Pyramid enclosure, suggesting that he may well have been the chief architect of this remarkable group of stone buildings. The pyramid started as a normal mastaba, but later more mastabas were added to it. Eventually, it consisted of six terraces, or steps, that rose 60 metres (200 ft) into the sky. The whole structure was originally clad with smooth white limestone.

The Step Pyramid, like the later pyramids, was both a royal tomb and a temple where the spirit (or ka) of the dead king could be worshipped.

Djoser's statue was found in a sealed chamber near the pyramid's north-east corner. Although the Step Pyramid was the first of the Egyptian pyramids, building it was clearly a huge effort that took a great amount of resources and thousands of workers. The cost and effort that went into building the structure shows how important the cult of the divine king was.

The Step Pyramid at Saqqara, the first pyramid, was begun in about 2630 BCE, making it the oldest stone structure of similar size in the world. Under the pyramid is Djoser's tomb. It had been robbed in ancient times, so the sarcophagus is now empty.

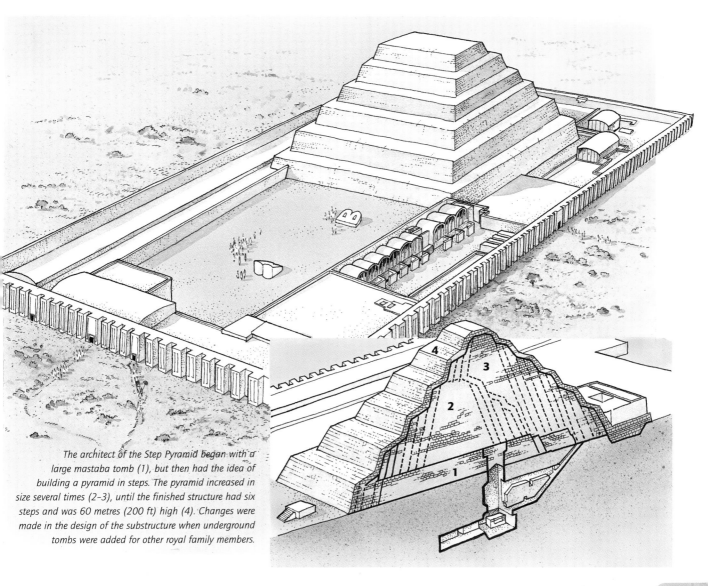

The architect of the Step Pyramid began with a large mastaba tomb (1), but then had the idea of building a pyramid in steps. The pyramid increased in size several times (2-3), until the finished structure had six steps and was 60 metres (200 ft) high (4). Changes were made in the design of the substructure when underground tombs were added for other royal family members.

THE OLD KINGDOM

During the Fourth Dynasty, members of the ruling royal family held the key positions in government. The first king of the dynasty was Snofru. He was supposed to have been a kind ruler. He was responsible for building at least two true (straight-sided) pyramids for himself. One of the pyramids is known as the 'Bent Pyramid', because halfway up its height it changes angle abruptly.

During Snofru's reign, the Egyptians built a fortified town at Buhen in Nubia to the south. From there, they were able to exploit the Nubian gold fields and to control trade routes into Africa. Unlike Snofru, the next ruler, Khufu, who is best-known as the builder of the Great Pyramid at Giza, was remembered as a cruel and mean ruler. Later, the pharaohs Khephren and Menkaura also built huge pyramids at Giza.

Tombs of queens, princesses and officials were built around the pyramids. Human sacrifice had once been practiced during royal burial rites but was now abandoned. Statues of the Fourth Dynasty kings show them as serene figures, who were not only absolute rulers but also living

gods. However, many only ruled for a short period. Some experts think that might mean that they died in wars with rivals. The peaceful appearance of the statues may be misleading.

The Old Kingdom was a high point in Egyptian art. Beautiful statues and reliefs

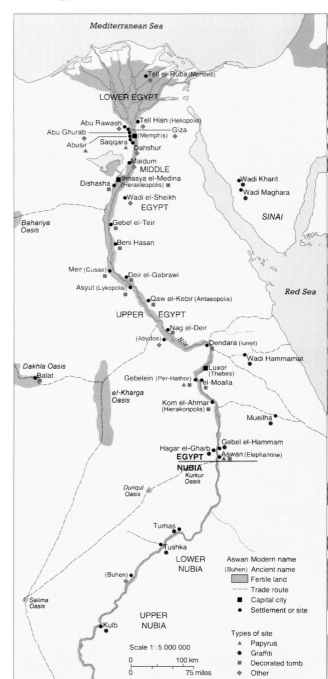

Egypt and Nubia in the Old Kingdom and the First Intermediate Period. The major Fourth- and Fifth-Dynasty sites are clustered near the capital, Memphis. Lower Nubia was almost uninhabited until it was settled by the "C–Group" during the Sixth Dynasty.

Old Kingdom and First Intermediate Period

Papyrus sites Papyrus was probably first used for writing on in the Old Kingdom. Old Kingdom papyri include legal documents and temple records.

Graffiti sites These consist of names and titles scratched on rocks by members of Egyptian mining and trading expeditions. Most date from the Sixth Dynasty.

Decorated tomb sites By the late Old Kingdom, important officials were building themselves elaborate tombs in provincial cemeteries. This shows the increasing wealth and independence of the regions. The decoration in First Intermediate Period tombs is crude compared with Old Kingdom art.

(raised images) were carved in stone. Subjects like mathematics, astronomy and engineering flourished during the Old Kingdom. Perhaps the complex job of building a pyramid helped to promote both artistic and scientific advances.

Pyramid Building

The pyramids required a huge amount of labour to build. Some of the builders belonged to a permanent workforce of craftsmen. Many others were peasants who worked on royal projects for the two months of the year when the fields were flooded and it was impossible for them to farm. Up to 100,000 men may have worked for as many as twenty flood seasons to build a single pyramid. To build such enormous structures required a stable and rich country as well as a well-organised workforce. The vast civil service that developed to cope with the pyramid building remained an important feature of ancient Egyptian civilisation.

Pyramids built during the Fifth Dynasty were smaller in scale than earlier pyramids. Several kings built magnificent stone temples to the sun god Ra. The pyramid of the last king of the Fifth Dynasty, Wenis, was the first to have the famous spells known as the Pyramid Texts carved onto it. The spells were meant to help the king become a god in the afterlife and to help him take his place among the stars.

Rise of the Nomarchs

In the Sixth Dynasty, royal power declined. The government was no longer controlled by princes. Important officials continued to build lavish tombs for themselves, but they described themselves with humble titles such as 'Keeper of the King's Nail Clippings'.

All the land in Egypt originally belonged to the king but, over time, the kings gave it away to support temples and reward officials. Estates could belong to the cults of gods or to dead ancestors. This meant that little or no tax was paid on any wealth the estates gathered. Over time, royal wealth disappeared. The kings' political power was also threatened by the gradual rise in the power of the nomarchs. The office of nomarch had started to pass from father to son.

The Slide Into Chaos

Pepy II, who reigned for more than 90 years, was the last ruler of the Sixth Dynasty. After a number of poor flood seasons caused famine and some nomarchs declared themselves kings, Egypt started to split into a number of smaller states. Chaos followed. During the First Intermediate Period poverty and violence became the norm, as a later 13th Dynasty poem summed up, 'All happiness has disappeared, the land is bowed down in misery'.

THE MIDDLE KINGDOM

The First Intermediate Period ended only after nearly a century of upheaval. A king from Thebes reunited Egypt. Under Nebhepetra Mentuhotep II, the kingdom grew wealthy again. Once more, the government organised large-scale building projects. The reign of the 11th Dynasty was short, however. After just two more kings, power changed hands. Thanks either to violence or a peaceful succession, the throne passed to the vizier, Amenemhet.

Amenemhet founded a new dynasty, the 12th, which ruled from a new capital city called Itjawy (near el-Lisht). He selected the location to give him a more central power base. To keep control, he re-organised the administration. He kept the nomarchs, who had supported his seizure of power, but took away power from the regional governors. After he had ruled for 20 years, he made his son, Senwosret, his co-ruler. Egyptian territory expanded under their rule into Nubia, and they constructed a long chain of forts along the Nile. Later 12th Dynasty rulers followed Amenemhet's example. Amenemhet was murdered while his son was away fighting the Libyans, but the system of government was strong enough to prevent the country falling into civil disorder.

The Careworn Kings

The greatest of the 12th Dynasty kings was Senwosret III. He conquered more of neighbouring Nubia than any of his ancestors and spread Egyptian influence as far north as Palestine. He took away power from the nomarchs and increased the power of the central government.

Although the pyramids from this period were poorly built, the artwork of the 12th Dynasty was of a very high quality. It also showed a different idea of kingship. Statues of Senwosret III and his son, Amenemhet III, show them with very tired looking faces. Their faces are much more human-like than the god-images of the earlier dynasties, which had set out to illustrate the divine nature of the kings. Even the writings from the Middle Kingdom stressed how hard it was for the king to rule.

The Reign of the Hyksos

The last ruler of the 12th Dynasty was a queen, Nefrusobek, which suggests the royal family had probably died out because of the lack of a male heir. During the 13th Dynasty, Egypt continued to prosper, although no king stayed in power for very long. It may be that the real power lay in

---

SELECTED KINGS OF THE MIDDLE KINGDOM, 2040–1640 BCE

11th Dynasty 2040–1991

Nebhepetra Mentuhotep II 2061–2010

Mentuhotep III 2010–1998

Mentuhotep IV 1998–1991

12th Dynasty 1991–1783

Amenemhet I 1991–1962

Senwosret I 1971–1926

Amenemhet II 1929–1892

Senwosret II 1897–1878

Senwosret III 1878–1841

Amenemhet III 1844–1797

Amenemhet IV 1799–1787

Queen Nefrusobek 1787–1783

13th Dynasty 1783–1640

About 70 kings, most with short reigns. Best known include:

Sobekhotep I c.1750

Hor c.1748?

Sobekhotep III c.1745

Neferhotep I c.1741–1730

Sobekhotep IV c.1730–1720

Sobekhotep V c.1720–1715

Aya c.1704–1690

Second Intermediate Period

1640–1550 BCE

14th Dynasty

Minor kings contemporary with dynasties 13 and 15

15th Dynasty

Hyksos kings ruling from Avaris:

Salitis

Sheshi

Khian

Apophis c.1585–1542

Khamudi c.1542–1532

16th Dynasty

Minor Hyksos kings contemporary with 15th Dynasty

17th Dynasty 1640–1550

Numerous Theban kings. The best known are:

Inyotef V c.1640–1635

Seqenenra c.1560–1555

Kamose 1555–1550

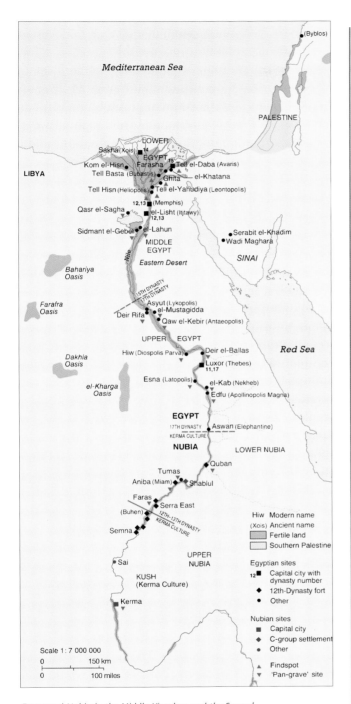

Egypt and Nubia in the Middle Kingdom and the Second Intermediate Period. The map shows capital cities and changing centres of power during the 11th to 17th Dynasties. These include areas of Nubia controlled by Egypt's line of forts along the Nile, and major sites of the Nubian culture groups.

Middle Kingdom and Second Intermediate Period

Find spots The finds include bronze weapons and distinctive pottery of the Middle Bronze Age culture of Palestine and those parts of Egypt settled by the Hyksos.

Dynasty capitals The centres of power often changed with dynasties. The local god of a dynastic capital became an important deity.

'Pan-grave' sites The 'Pan-grave' people were nomads from the Eastern Desert who served as mercenary soldiers in Egypt and Nubia.

12th Dynasty forts and 'C-group' settlements – The Egyptians built forts to control the 'C-group' culture people from the Lower Nubia and to create a buffer zone against the fierce 'Kerma culture' people of Kush (Upper Nubia). In the Second Intermediate Period, the Princes of Kush ruled Lower Nubia and attacked Upper Egypt.

the hands of officials like the vizier. Rival dynasties started to challenge for power. One of them was a foreign dynasty known as the Hyksos. They founded the 15th Dynasty.

The Hyksos had originated in Palestine but moved south to Egypt, where they settled in the Delta. They lived according to their own laws in their own communities. The Hyksos kings soon expanded their power until they controlled all of Egypt. They also made an alliance with Kush, an area of Upper Nubia, which was also ruled by local princes.

During the Second Intermediate Period, local rulers still held power in much of the Nile Valley. The Hyksos kings tolerated them, as long as they continued to pay tribute (a tax) to the Hyksos in their capital of Avaris. A new dynasty of Theban kings arose to the south of the delta. They, too, paid tribute to the Hyksos, but they had ambitions to free Egypt from foreign rule.

A Theban king named Seqenenra led an army against the Hyksos, but he died after a battle. His mummy showed terrible axe wounds. His successor, Kamose, continued the fight against the Hyksos and the Nubians of Kush.

Map labels:

(Byblos)

Mediterranean Sea

PALESTINE

LOWER EGYPT

Sakha (Xois) 14
Kom el-Hisn · Farasha · 15 · Tell el-Daba (Avaris)
Tell Basta (Bubastis) · Ghita · el-Khatana
Tell Hisn (Heliopolis) · Tell el-Yahudiya (Leontopolis)
(Memphis) 12,13
Qasr el-Sagha · el-Lisht (Itjtawy) 12,13
Sidmant el-Gebel · el-Lahun
LIBYA
MIDDLE EGYPT
Serabit el-Khadim
Wadi Maghara
SINAI
Nile
Eastern Desert
Bahariya Oasis
Farafra Oasis
15TH DYNASTY 17TH DYNASTY
Asyut (Lykopolis)
Deir Rifa · el-Mustagidda
Qaw el-Kebir (Antaeopolis)
UPPER EGYPT
Dakhla Oasis
Hiw (Diospolis Parva) · Deir el-Ballas
Red Sea
Luxor (Thebes) 11,17
el-Kharga Oasis
Esna (Latopolis) · el-Kab (Nekheb)
Edfu (Apollinopolis Magna)
EGYPT
17TH DYNASTY · Aswan (Elephantine)
KERMA CULTURE
NUBIA
LOWER NUBIA
Quban
Tumas
Aniba (Miam) · Shablul
Faras
Serra East
(Buhen) · 12TH–13TH DYNASTY / KERMA CULTURE
Semna
Sai
UPPER NUBIA
KUSH (Kerma Culture)
Kerma

Scale 1 : 7 000 000
0 — 150 km
0 — 100 miles

Hiw Modern name
(Xois) Ancient name
Fertile land
Southern Palestine
Egyptian sites
12■ Capital city with dynasty number
◆ 12th-Dynasty fort
● Other
Nubian sites
■ Capital city
◆ C-group settlement
● Other
▲ Findspot
▼ 'Pan-grave' site

THE NEW KINGDOM

It was the first king of the 18th Dynasty, a ruler named Ahmose, who finally got rid of the Hyksos from Egypt and the Prince of Kush from Lower Nubia. As a consequence of Ahmose's victories, by the end of the reign, Egypt controlled an area that stretched from Palestine to Upper Nubia.

Thutmose I led the armies of Egypt farther north than they had ever gone. He founded an empire in Palestine and Syria. His successor, Thutmose II, died young. Thutmose II's widow and sister, Hatshepsut, acted as regent for the boy king, Thutmose III, her husband's son by a lower-ranking wife. After several years, she declared herself king. Hatshepsut claimed the equivalent power to a male pharaoh. Statues show her wearing the traditional clothing of male kings. Hatshepsut's reign appears to have been peaceful and prosperous. Images in her beautiful temple at Deir el-Bahri show an expedition returning to her kingdom from a land the Egyptians named Punt (probably in present-day Eritrea) with valuable goods such as incense trees.

After Hatshepsut's death, Thutmose III fought a series of battles to consolidate Egypt's rule in both Palestine and Syria. Tribute paid from across the empire and gold from Nubia made Egypt the wealthiest place anywhere in the ancient world. The 18th Dynasty kings used this wealth to build magnificent temples to a range of both local and more widespread deities. The most popular god was Amon. His temple at Karnak in Thebes became the largest in Egypt.

Akhenaten, the Sun King

The dominance of Amon was challenged temporarily during the reign of one of the 18th Dynasty's most remarkable rulers, Akhenaten. Akhenaten's father, Amonhotep III, built more lavishly than his ancestors as the remains of his palace at Thebes show. His son, Amonhotep IV, changed his name to Akhenaten and made Aten (the sun disk) the main god of Egypt. Moving his capital to el-Amarna, he declared Aten the only god and closed down the temples of other gods.

Akhenaten broke with tradition. He allowed himself to be pictured by artists and sculptors in informal family scenes, kissing his beautiful wife, Nefertiti, or playing with his daughters.

Akhenaten's rule was unpopular, and during the reign of Tutankhamon, the new capital was abandoned and the old religious order restored.

Ramesses II's army in camp. Chariot horses are tethered in rows waiting to be fed and watered, while close by a chariot is being repaired. A company of foot soldiers is drilled by its standard-bearer, and the king's pet lion is being taken for a walk. None of the soldiers has a helmet; thick wigs or bushy hairstyles cushioned the head from the enemy's blows. The weapons shown include shields made of cowhide stretched on wooden frames and a bow made from two antelope horns lashed together.

Capital Cities of the New Kingdom and Later

Thebes The New Kingdom religious capital and the royal burial place.

Memphis Administrative capital for most of the 18th Dynasty and early 19th Dynasty.

El-Amarna New capital begun in year five of Akhenaten's rule. Abandoned 15 years later under Tutankhamon.

Pi-Ramesses Built under Ramesses II. The probable site is the Qantir district near Tell el-Daba in the northeast of the Delta.

Tanis Capital and burial place of kings of the 21st and 22nd Dynasties.

Bubastis City of origin and religious capital of the 22nd Dynasty.

Leontopolis Capital and probable burial place of some 23rd Dynasty rulers.

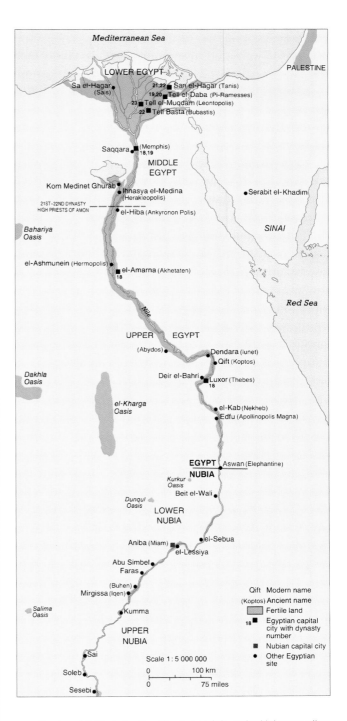

Egypt and Nubia in the New Kingdom and the early Third Intermediate Period. During the latter period, the High Priests of Amon at Thebes controlled the area between Aswan and el-Hiba while the kings of the 21st and 22nd Dynasties ruled the north. The sites marked in Nubia are towns or temples built by the Egyptians during the New Kingdom.

Akhenaten's name was carefully scratched off any monuments where it had been engraved. The capital at el-Armana was abandoned.

The Ramessid Pharaohs

After Tutankhamon, who died when he was still a young teenager, the throne passed to a series of officials. The third was a general, Ramesses, who founded the 19th Dynasty. His son, Seti I, was a strong ruler but it was his grandson, Ramesses II (1290–1224 BCE), who became one of the greatest of all the Egyptian pharaohs. He ruled for 66 years and erected more buildings and huge statues than any other Egyptian king.

Under the Ramessids, Egypt was prosperous, but its borders were increasingly under threat. The Libyans and other invaders threatened Ramesses II's successor, Merneptah. Ramesses III, the second king of the 20th Dynasty (1196–1070), fought land and sea battles against invaders who were known to the Egyptians as the Sea Peoples. During the 20th Dynasty, Egypt's power started to decline as the power of the priesthood at Thebes started to rival that of the king.

EGYPT AND ITS NEIGHBOURS

The Egyptians believed that they were more important than all the other races with whom they came into contact. When foreigners appeared in Egyptian art, it was usually to show them in humble situations, such as paying tribute or as bound prisoners. The Nubians to the south, the Libyans to the west and the 'vile Asiatics' to the east were pictured on the pharaoh's footstool or on the sole of his sandals, so that he symbolically trod on Egypt's enemies. In reality, however, some of Egypt's North African and West Asian neighbours were potential threats to Egypt.

Legacy of the Hyksos

Toward the end of the Middle Kingdom, large numbers of Asiatic peoples were allowed to settle in Egypt. Their presence had made it easier for the Hyksos kings to take power. The new immigrants brought with them new bronze-working techniques, as well as improved types of looms and potter's wheels. They also introduced new types of weapons, as well as the tactic of fighting from horse-drawn chariots.

The Theban kings of the 17th and 18th Dynasties drove the Hyksos from Egypt into Palestine and Syria, which were then divided into small states, each with its own ruling prince. The Egyptians easily terrorised these princes into acknowledging the reign of the pharaoh and paying tribute to the Egyptian treasury. Northern Syria, however, was beyond the reach of the Egyptian kings. It belonged to the powerful kingdom of Mitanni (Naharin), an Indo–Iranian empire based in northern Mesopotamia.

Mitanni and the Hittites

Thutmose I attacked Mitanni and led his Egyptian army as far north as the Euphrates River. He celebrated his victory with a great elephant hunt at Niya. Keeping control of this new addition to the empire was troublesome, however. Egypt often had to send an army to recapture rebel states or to threaten Mitanni. Thutmose III fought 14 major campaigns in Palestine and Syria to restore order

among Egypt's tributary states. Inscriptions in the temple of Karnak show some of the loot carried off during these campaigns, and a relief shows exotic plants, birds and animals collected for the pharaoh in Syria.

Eventually, Egypt and Mitanni came to a relatively peaceful coexistence. The pharaoh Thutmose IV and his son, Amonhotep III, both married princesses from Mitanni and sent wedding gifts of gold north to the rulers of Mitanni. Under the reign of Akhenaten, however, the pharaoh was so busy with his new religion that he largely ignored foreign affairs. Once again the empire of Mitanni broke away from Egyptian control.

The Hittites

By the 19th Dynasty, Mitanni had declined and Egypt's main rival in the Near East was now the Hittite Empire. The Hittites were a war-like people whose homeland was the mountains of Anatolia, in modern-day Turkey, more than 965 kilometres (600 mi) north from Thebes. The Hittites fought with Seti I and Ramesses II for control of Syria.

The battle of Qadesh in about 1285 BCE pitched the forces of Egypt under Ramesses II

Northern Frontiers of the Egyptian Empire

1. Farthest point reached by Thutmose I.

2. Frontier at the end of Thutmose III's reign.

3. Frontier in year 7 of Amonhotep II.

4. Frontier under Thutmose IV.

5. Frontier under Tutankhamon.

6. Frontier in year 21 of Ramesses II.

Egypt and the Near East (c.1530–1190 BCE). Egypt traded with Cyprus, Crete and Mycenaean Greece. The great Near Eastern powers were the Mitannis, Hittites, Babylonians and Assyrians. The numbers on the map refer to the box above.

against the Hittites led by Muwatalli II for control of Syria. Ramesses II won the battle – the first in history for which there is a contemporary account – but only a few years later he signed a peace treaty with the Hittites and married a Hittite princess. The Hittite empire was destroyed in the 12th century BCE by a mass arrival of migrants identified as the Sea Peoples. Egypt itself narrowly avoided being overthrown by the Sea Peoples, but lost all of its Near Eastern empire.

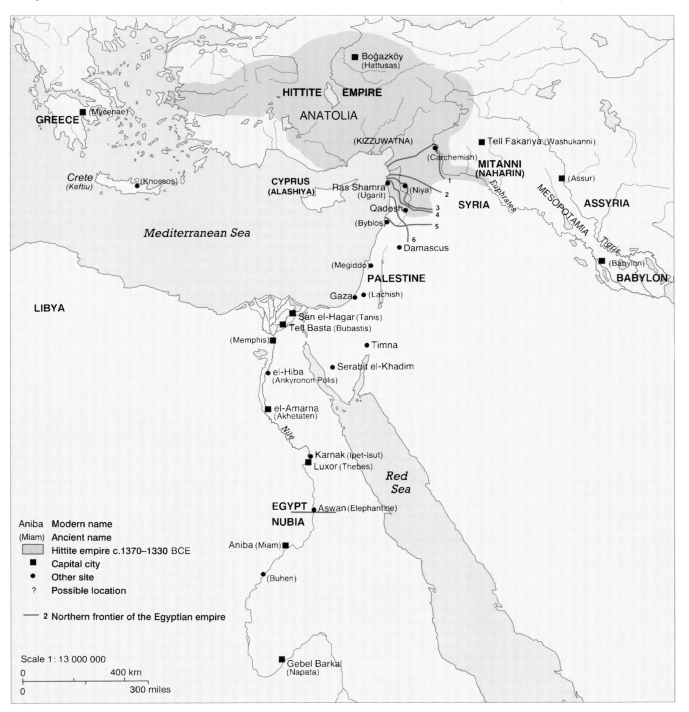

Aniba	Modern name
(Miam)	Ancient name
	Hittite empire c.1370–1330 BCE
■	Capital city
●	Other site
?	Possible location

—— 2 Northern frontier of the Egyptian empire

Scale 1 : 13 000 000

0   400 km

0   300 miles

EGYPT DIVIDED

By the end of the 20th Dynasty, Egypt had lost much of its outlying territory. It had lost Nubia to the south as well as the Near Eastern empire in what are now Syria and Lebanon. The kings of the late 20th Dynasty, based in their Delta capital, had little influence even over Upper Egypt. The High Priest of Amon, who controlled the huge wealth of the temple of Karnak in Thebes, was the effective ruler of the south. The office of high priest had by now become hereditary – it was always held by a member of the same family.

The Third Intermediate Period

With the death of the last 20th Dynasty ruler, the so-called Third Intermediate Period began when a king called Smendes claimed power in the north of the country. He established his capital at Tanis in the north-east Delta. The 21st Dynasty kings brought statues, obelisks and decorated blocks created during earlier reigns to decorate the new capital.

The dynasty of high priests, based in Thebes, recognised the claims of the 21st Dynasty kings to power, but continued to effectively rule the south. Soon, however, the pharaohs' power in the Delta region was also disputed.

Dynastic Rivalries

During the late New Kingdom, a large number of settlers from neighbouring Libya arrived in Lower Egypt, where they became a powerful political force. The first king of the 22nd

A Legacy of Warring Kings

The Victory Stela of Piye From c.730 BCE the Theban area was under the power of Nubian kings from Napata. One of these kings, Piye, recorded his victorious campaign in Egypt on a stela set up in the temple of Amon at Napata, southern Nubia. The stela is our main source for the history of this period.

Cities taken by Tefnakhte The cause of Piye's campaign was the expanding power of Tefnakhte of Sais, in the western Delta, who called himself 'Chief of the West'. The cities taken over by Tefnakhte are listed on Piye's victory stela.

Dynasty came from a family of Libyan descent. Shoshenq I was a strong ruler who won back a number of Egypt's former territories in Palestine.

By this time, the Jews had established the kingdom of Judah in the region. Shoshenq attacked Judah and removed a lot of treasure from the temple at Jerusalem. Details about the conquests were recorded in the buildings that Shoshenq added to the temple at Karnak. To protect his power base, Shoshenq installed his son as the high priest at Thebes, bringing the whole of Egypt once again under the control of a single dynasty. The unification lasted for about one century. Then, rebellions in the south started and a rival dynasty, the 23rd, was established in the Delta.

Egypt started to split into small areas, each with its own local ruler who called himself king. Two of the most important of these kings were the rulers of Hermopolis and Herakleopolis. King Orsokon IV of the 23rd Dynasty tried to take control of the south by getting rid of the

SELECTED KINGS OF THE THIRD INTERMEDIATE PERIOD 1070–712 BCE

21st Dynasty 1070–945	22nd Dynasty 945–712	23rd Dynasty c.828–712	24th Dynasty 724–712
Smendes 1070–1044	Shoshenq I 945–924	Rulers of Thebes, Hermopolis, Herakleopolis, Leontopolis and Tanis. The order of these kings is unknown and some ruled at the same time. They include:	Rulers of Sais:
Amenemnisu 1044–1040	Osorkon II 924–909		Tefnakhte 724–717
Psusennes I 1040–992	Takelot I 909–?		Bocchoris 717–712
Amenemope 993–984	Shoshenq II ?–883		
Osorkon I 984–978	Osorkon III 883–855	Pedubaste I 828–803	**25th Dynasty 770–712**
Siamun 978–959	Takelot II 860–835	Orsokon IV 777–749	Ruling Nubia and the Theban area:
Psusennes II 959–945	Shoshenq III 835–783	Peftjauawybast 740–725	Kashta 770–750
			Piye 750–712

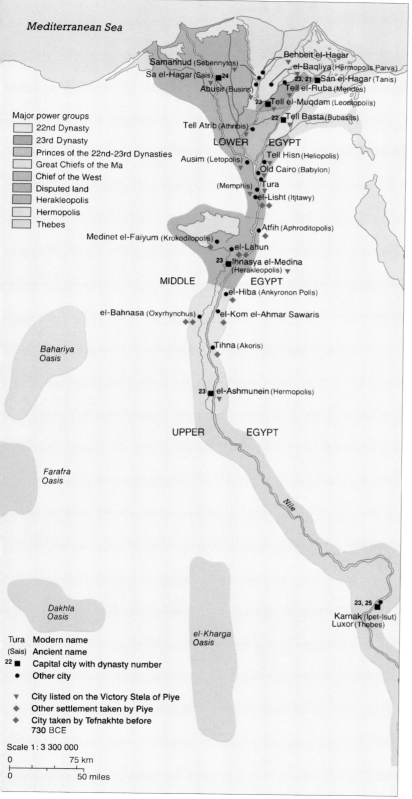

Major power groups
- 22nd Dynasty
- 23rd Dynasty
- Princes of the 22nd-23rd Dynasties
- Great Chiefs of the Ma
- Chief of the West
- Disputed land
- Herakleopolis
- Hermopolis
- Thebes

Mediterranean Sea

Samannud (Sebennytos)
Sa el-Hagar (Sais)   24
Abusir (Busiris)
Behbeit el-Hagar
el-Baqliya (Hermopolis Parva)
San el-Hagar (Tanis)   23, 21
Tell el-Ruba (Mendes)
23   Tell el-Muqdam (Leontopolis)
22   Tell Basta (Bubastis)
Tell Atrib (Athribis)

LOWER EGYPT

Ausim (Letopolis)
Tell Hisn (Heliopolis)
Old Cairo (Babylon)
(Memphis)   Tura
el-Lisht (Itjtawy)

Atfih (Aphroditopolis)

Medinet el-Faiyum (Krokodilopolis)
el-Lahun
23   Ihnasya el-Medina (Herakleopolis)

MIDDLE EGYPT

el-Hiba (Ankyronon Polis)
el-Bahnasa (Oxyrhynchus)
el-Kom el-Ahmar Sawaris

Bahariya Oasis

Tihna (Akoris)

23   el-Ashmunein (Hermopolis)

UPPER EGYPT

Farafra Oasis

Nile

Dakhla Oasis

23, 25   Karnak (Ipet-Isut)
Luxor (Thebes)

el-Kharga Oasis

Tura   Modern name
(Sais)   Ancient name
22 ■   Capital city with dynasty number
●   Other city
▼   City listed on the Victory Stela of Piye
◆   Other settlement taken by Piye
◆   City taken by Tefnakhte before 730 BCE

Scale 1 : 3 300 000
0   75 km
0   50 miles

by-then hereditary office of the high priest of Amon. He did this by making his daughter high priestess. The high priestess was supposed to be the bride of the god Amon. This meant that she could not marry a man – and therefore she could not found a dynasty that would rival that of the royal family.

Kings Out of Nubia

To the south, the kings of Napata now ruled all of Nubia. Although they were Nubian by birth, the Napatans had adopted Egyptian culture and religion. They built pyramids and worshipped Amon. One of the 25th Dynasty Nubian rulers, Kashta, took control of the region between Aswan and Thebes.

Kashta's successor, Piye, invaded Upper Egypt on the pretext that he was restoring order and the proper worship of the gods. Egyptian practices and deities were highly popular among the Nubians. Nubian rulers adopted many aspects of Egyptian culture, including building royal tombs in the shape of pyramids.

Piye forced the high priestess at Thebes to adopt his sister as her successor. He defeated the local ruler of Hermopolis and led his armies as far north as Memphis. After a fierce battle, King Piye entered the city, where he gave thanks for his victory in the temple of Ptah.

Tefnakhte, a chieftain who ruled the western Delta, was among the Egyptian rulers who had to acknowledge the rule of Piye and send him tribute in the form of payments of gold and other treasure. But after the Nubian king returned south, Tefnakhte continued to dominate the Delta. He was the first 24th Dynasty ruler of Sais.

Egypt in the late Third Intermediate Period. All the major power groups and their capitals are shown. The Great Chiefs of the Ma were Libyans. The exact boundary between the territories ruled by the local kings of Hermopolis and Herakleopolis is uncertain.

THE LAST EGYPTIAN RULERS

The next 25th Dynasty king after Piye was Shabaka. He defeated the pharaoh in Sais who claimed rule over the Delta and destroyed all other opposition. Shabaka then ruled a united kingdom of Egypt and Napata from Memphis. Reunification brought a period of renewed prosperity to Egypt. It ended as the whole region entered a period of great turmoil, which saw great empires rise and fall throughout the whole of West Asia.

The Assyrian Conquest of Egypt

In the seventh century BCE, the Assyrians of Mesopotamia were trying to expand their empire westwards into Palestine. Egypt formed a defensive alliance with the kingdom of Judah there, which earned it the hostility of the Assyrians. They invaded Egypt. Initially the invasion failed but, sometime around 671 BCE, the Assyrian king Esarhaddon captured the important city of Memphis.

With the Assyrians in control, the 25th Dynasty king Taharqa fled south to Napata, and Egypt found itself forced to pay tribute to the Assyrians. In return for acknowledging the superiority of the Assyrians, the local ruler of Sais, Necho, was allowed to retain the title of king. He was killed fighting Tantamani, Taharqa's successor.

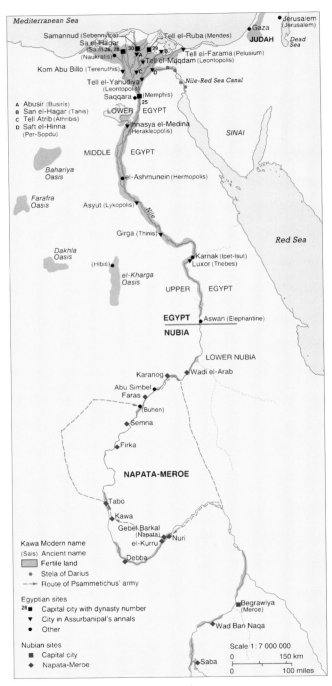

Egypt and the kingdom of Napata-Meroe, united under Shabaka before the Assyrian conquest. Meroe became the Nubian capital in around 591 BCE. At its peak, Meroe controlled territory that reached as far as Lake Chad on the border of modern-day Nigeria, Niger and Chad. The kingdom of Meroe endured until the fourth century CE.

Conquest in the Late Period

The annals of Assurbanipal This Assyrian king left detailed records of his wars. He lists the Egyptian cities whose rulers paid homage to him. These local rulers are described as kings, showing how divided Egypt had become.

The route of Psammetichus's Army The route most likely taken by Psammetichus II when he invaded Napata in 591 BCE. Evidence for the route comes from the graffiti left by his army. Many of the soldiers were Greek mercenaries.

Stelae of Darius The Persian king Darius I completed a canal begun by Necho II. The canal linked a branch of the River Nile to the Red Sea. Darius set up four stelae recording this achievement along the banks of the canal.

The next Assyrian king, Assurbanipal, pushed Tantamani back to Napata and sacked Thebes. Necho's son, Psammetichus, was left as a puppet ruler in the Delta and waited for an opportunity to take control if the Assyrians found themselves distracted by trouble in other parts of their empire. When Psammetichus finally got his chance, he seized it. He drove the Assyrians from Egypt, reclaimed the throne for the Saite 26th Dynasty and made himself king of Egypt.

Egypt Allies with Greece

Under the Saite kings of the 26th Dynasty, art and literature flourished in Egypt. The country was rarely at peace, however, as the balance of power shifted throughout West Asia. Babylon in Mesopotamia had risen to become a greater power than its neighbour Assyria. In 601 BCE, the Egyptian pharaoh Necho II had to defeat an attempted invasion led by the Babylonian ruler Nebuchadnezzar.

The next king, Psammetichus II, led an army deep into Nubia to intimidate the ruler of Napata. His successor, Apries, was deposed by an Egyptian general, Amasis. By this time, there were many Greeks serving in the Egyptian army and Amasis encouraged Greeks to establish a trading post at Naukratis, on a branch of the Nile in the west of the Delta.

The Persian Invasion

By the late sixth century BCE, Persia (modern-day Iran) had become the main power in West Asia. In 525 BCE, the Persian ruler Cambyses II invaded Egypt. He was helped in his conquest when the commander of the Egyptians' Greek allies switched sides to support the invaders. Cambyses successfully overthrew the Egyptian pharaoh, Psammetichus III, to become the first ruler of the 27th Dynasty, known as the First Persian Period.

Cambyses shocked the ancient world with the brutality and cruelty he showed towards his conquered subjects. He also showed contempt for the Egyptians' local deities, although he adopted the title and traditions of the pharaohs. His successor, Darius I, was a more moderate pharaoh, but the Egyptians nevertheless resented Persian rule. As a result, there were a number of rebellions against Persian rule, led by a series of Egyptian dynasties. None was successful for very long.

Persian rule in Egypt lasted until the late fourth century BCE. Then the young king of Macedon in Greece, Alexander the Great, conquered the whole of the Persian Empire. As part of his campaign he captured Persian naval bases farther north before marching in triumph into Egypt, where he was heralded as a saviour by the Egyptians.

GREEK AND ROMAN RULE

When Alexander the Great died in 323 BCE, his mighty empire stretched across Asia to modern India. It soon started to break up. Ptolemy, a Macedonian general, brought Alexander's body to Egypt and built a tomb for him in the new city of Alexandria, founded by the emperor himself in the Delta. In 304 BCE, Ptolemy declared himself king of Egypt, beginning a dynasty that ruled for more than 250 years. The male rulers were all known as Ptolemy.

Artists and scholars were encouraged to come to Alexandria, where Ptolemy established a large library. Many Greeks and Macedonians were also given parcels of land in Egypt. The Ptolemies almost always appointed Greek rather than Egyptian officials.

A Murderous Family

It was usual for Ptolemaic kings to marry their sisters. The royal ladies often acted as co-rulers with their husband–brothers. There were many power struggles within the family. Many of the rulers seized or kept hold of power by murdering their relatives to prevent opposition.

Although there were some rebellions against Greek rule in Upper Egypt, the Ptolemies tried to keep their Egyptian subjects happy by building splendid temples to their Egyptian gods.

By the first century BCE, Rome had become the greatest power in the ancient world. The Romans set their sights on Egypt, which they wanted for its gold and grain.

Queen Cleopatra VII

In 48 BCE, the great Roman general Julius Caesar intervened in an Egyptian civil war to support Cleopatra as ruler. Cleopatra was the first Ptolemy to learn Egyptian (the others had spoken Greek). Caesar was attracted by Cleopatra's wit and beauty. They had a son.

Following Julius Caesar's murder in Rome, another Roman general, Mark Antony, also fell in love with Cleopatra. Antony and Cleopatra ruled until they were attacked by Julius Caesar's heir, Octavian (Augustus). Defeated, they were forced to take their own lives.

Roman Rule

As a province of the Roman Empire, Egypt was now ruled by prefects, who were appointed by the emperor. Temples continued to be built to the Egyptian gods, however. The worship of the

Desert Finds and Roman Roads

Papyrus Sites Sites at which papyri or ostraca written on in ancient Greek were found. They include plays and poems, books on medicine and mathematics, as well as many personal letters. Many great works of Greek and Roman literature survive only in copies that were preserved by the hot, dry climate of Egypt. Papyrus production was a major industry in Alexandria.

Roman Way-Stations The Romans built a road network in the Eastern Desert. Way-stations were provided with water supplies to make it easier for expeditions to cross the desert. The Romans quarried granite and porphyry, a stone used to make statues and vessels, and mined for emeralds. The roads led to ports on the Red Sea. The Persian-built canal linking the River Nile to the Red Sea was improved under the emperor Trajan.

SELECTED RULERS OF THE GRECO–ROMAN PERIOD, 332 BCE–395 CE

Macedonian Dynasty 332–304

Alexander the Great 332–323
Philip Arrhidaeus 323–316
Alexander IV 316–304

Ptolemaic Dynasty 304–30

The reigns of most later Ptolemies were interrupted by civil wars.

Ptolemy I 304–284
Ptolemy II 285–246
Ptolemy III 246–221
Ptolemy IV 221–205
Ptolemy V 205–180
Ptolemy VI 180–164 & 163–145

Ptolemy VII 145
Ptolemy VIII 170–163 & 145–116
Queen Cleopatra III & Ptolemy IX 116–107
Queen Cleopatra III & Ptolemy X 107–88
Ptolemy IX 88–81
Queen Cleopatra IV 81–80
Ptolemy XI 80
Ptolemy XII 80–58 & 55–51

Ptolemy XIII 51–47
Ptolemy XIV 47–44
Queen Cleopatra VII 51–30

Roman Rule

30 BCE–395 CE
Rule by prefects appointed by the emperor.

goddess Isis actually spread throughout the empire. Greek and Roman settlers in Egypt also adopted some Egyptian burial customs.

However, native Egyptians had very little power in their country. They lived under Roman law and were taxed heavily so that most Egyptian people were forced to live in extreme poverty. The ancient Egyptian culture – some parts of which had existed for thousands of years – was finally destroyed when Christianity became the official religion of the Roman Empire in the fourth century CE.

Egypt in the Greco–Roman Period. During the Ptolemaic era most of the country's wealth was centred on Alexandria, the capital. Land reclamation schemes and improved irrigation transformed the Faiyum into a prosperous agricultural area. Many Greeks settled there. Group tombs full of gilded mummies have been found at Bahariya Oasis.

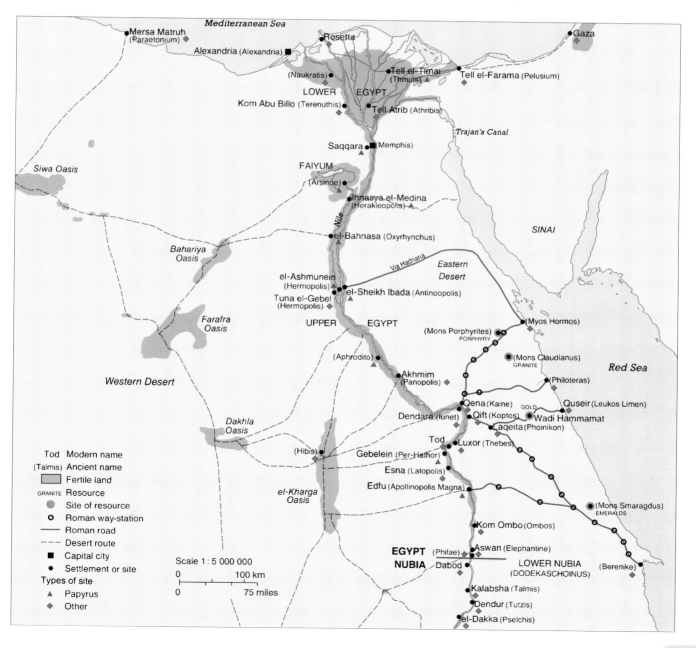

NUBIA

In most of ancient Nubia, the Nile Valley consisted of a narrow strip on either side of the river banks. Some Nubian groups settled in the few areas of land that were fertile enough to support crops and raise livestock. Other people lived as nomads in the deserts. During the Old Kingdom, the Egyptians often raided Lower Nubia to capture people and cattle. They also wanted to gain control of the profitable trade routes into Africa and the gold mines of the Nubian desert.

In the Middle Kingdom, Egypt conquered all of Lower Nubia as well as part of Upper Nubia (in present-day Sudan). The Egyptians tried to control their conquests by building a series of forts along the River Nile, mainly in the area of the Second and Third Cataracts. Egypt later lost control of Nubia, although some Egyptians continued to live there.

During the New Kingdom, Egypt once again conquered its southern neighbour. This time, instead of building forts, they built towns and temples. The population of Lower Nubia was very small by the end of the New Kingdom, perhaps as a result of years of drought.

From the Late Period, a native dynasty ruled the whole of Nubia. Influenced by the Egyptians, they continued to build temples and pyramids at their capitals in Napata and later Meroe. They built in the Egyptian style for hundreds of years. In the later Greco–Roman Period, a few temples to Egyptian and Nubian gods were built in Lower Nubia. One Nubian tribe, the Blemmyes, still worshipped the goddess Isis long after Egypt had become a Christian state.

Flooding of Nubia in Modern Times

The decision by the Egyptian government to build the new Aswan High Dam across the River Nile in the 1960s meant that much of what was Lower Nubia had to be flooded to create a giant reservoir, known as Lake Nasser. Before the flooding took place, however, the United Nations organised a huge salvage campaign, funded by international donations, to save all the area's main archaeological ruins. This involved digging up and recording every item at the ancient sites. The urgent project brought together an international team of archaeologists to save as much as they could of the Nubian heritage. In fact, the concentrated burst of activity also allowed them to make many exciting finds and to learn a lot of new information about life in ancient Nubia.

Many of the most important monuments were physically removed to positions safely above the waterline. Some temples, such as Abu Simbel and Amada, were simply dismantled stone-by-stone and rebuilt on higher ground in the same area. Others, such as Kalabsha, were rebuilt at entirely new sites. Some of the temples were even removed from their sites and re-erected outside Egypt. The temple of Dabod, for example, now stands in a park in Madrid. At the Metropolitan Museum of Art in New York, a new wing was built specifically to house the temple of Dendur.

Much of what was Lower Nubia is now flooded by Lake Nasser, the reservoir created by the building of the Aswan High Dam in the 1960s. Some old sites such as Abu Simbel were reconstructed in safe locations. Moving the temple at Old Kalabsha to a new site – New Kalabsha – involved dismantling, transporting and rebuilding some 13,000 blocks of stone. The original temple was the largest free-standing structure in all of Lower Nubia.

Dibeira E
Dibeira.

Buhen
Kor
Mirgissa (Iqen)

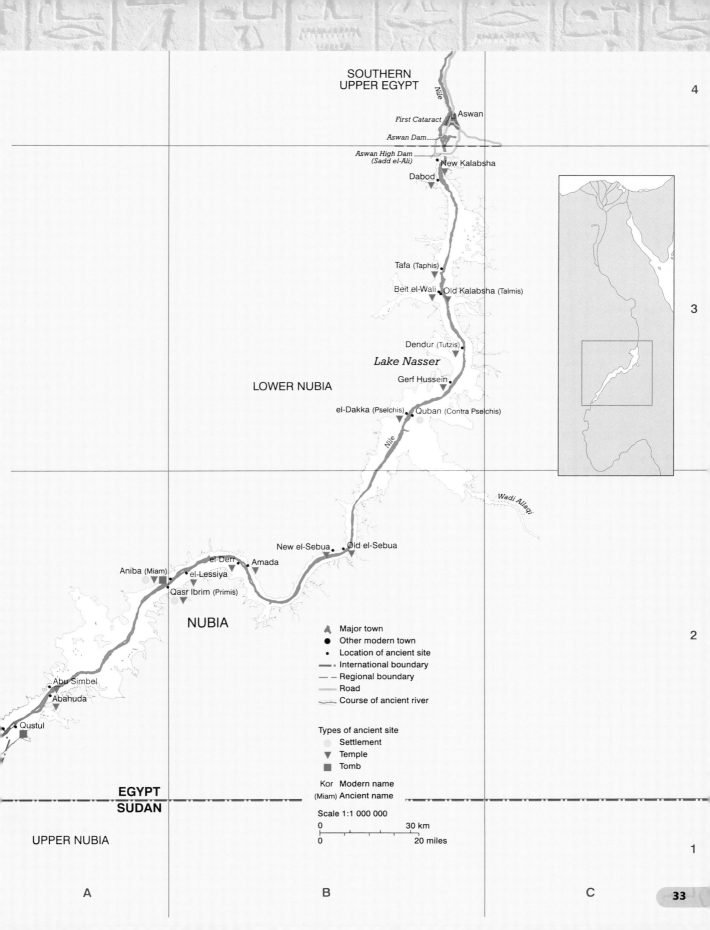

SOUTHERN
UPPER EGYPT

Nile

First Cataract
Aswan

Aswan Dam

Aswan High Dam
(Sadd el-Ali)
New Kalabsha

Dabod

Tafa (Taphis)

Beit el-Wali
Old Kalabsha (Talmis)

Dendur (Tutzis)

Lake Nasser

LOWER NUBIA

Gerf Hussein

el-Dakka (Pselchis)
Quban (Contra Pselchis)

Nile

Wadi Allaqi

New el-Sebua
Old el-Sebua

el-Derr
Amada

Aniba (Miam)
el-Lessiya

Qasr Ibrim (Primis)

NUBIA

Abu Simbel
Abahuda

Qustul

EGYPT
SUDAN

UPPER NUBIA

▲ Major town
● Other modern town
• Location of ancient site
▬·▬ International boundary
▬ ▬ Regional boundary
▬ Road
〰 Course of ancient river

Types of ancient site
⬤ Settlement
▼ Temple
■ Tomb

Kor   Modern name
(Miam) Ancient name

Scale 1:1 000 000
0   30 km
0   20 miles

4

3

2

1

A   B   C

Abu Simbel

Ramesses II built seven major temples in Nubia in the 19th Dynasty. The two most famous of these are the temples at Abu Simbel, known as the Great Temple and the Small Temple. They are built into a sandstone cliff.

Carved out inside the cliff are two pillared halls decorated with rock-cut reliefs. Some of the reliefs show the pharaoh in his chariot fighting the Hittites at Qadesh. Ramesses was very proud of his role in the victory and wanted to show off his military prowess.

The Great Temple was designed so that twice a year, during the summer and winter solstices, the rising sun would shine through its entrance and reach the inner part of the temple, lighting up the statues of the gods. In the beautiful Small Temple, the Great Royal Wife, Nefertari, is shown being crowned as a goddess.

The Rescue of the Temples

In the 1960s, the temples of Abu Simbel were threatened with destruction. They would have been submerged under the rising waters of Lake Nasser when the Aswan High Dam was built. In order to save them, people and governments across the world raised the sum of £25 million. The Great Temple was cut into 807 large blocks and the Small Temple into 235 blocks. Meanwhile, an artificial cliff was built 66 metres (215 ft) above the original site. The blocks were moved to the new site and put back together again exactly as before; they were covered by a huge concrete dome. The operation took four and a half years. Now Abu Simbel is not only a wonder of the ancient world but also a wonder of modern technology.

1 Terrace
2 Grand entrance with colossi
3 Great pillared hall
4 Side rooms
5 Small pillared hall
6 Anteroom
7 Sanctuary with niche for cult statues

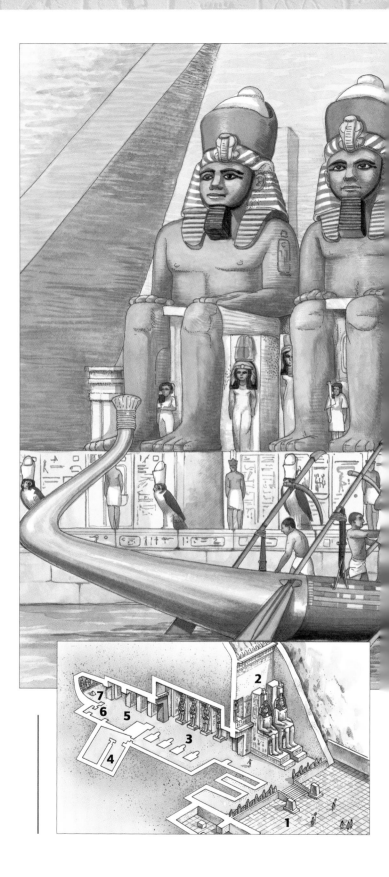

LEFT: A cutaway view showing the plan of the Great Temple. Most Egyptian temples had a walled forecourt, a grand entrance, one or more pillared (hypostyle) halls and a sanctuary that housed the cult statues.

ABOVE: Priests and a high official arrive at the Great Temple of Abu Simbel for the festival of the sun god. The most important festivals were on the two days of the year when the sun's rays shone through the entrance and along the main axis to the sanctuary. In ancient times the temples would have looked much more colourful than they do today. The rock-cut facade of the Great Temple has four 21-metre (70-ft) high statues (colossi) of Ramesses II. His mother, his chief wife and eight of his 140 children are shown on a much smaller scale at the feet of the statues.

SOUTHERN UPPER EGYPT

In ancient times the border between Egypt and Nubia lay at Biga. The island was submerged after the building of the Aswan High Dam. In the first four nomes, or districts, of Upper Egypt, the Nile Valley is narrow and the desert is very close to the river banks.

There was not much land to grow crops and vegetables, but the deserts were very rich in valuable minerals. Sandstone, granite, diorite, quartzite and steatite (used for buildings and statues) were quarried from sites close to Aswan. An amethyst mine was also located in the same area. Gold was found in both the Eastern and Nubian Deserts.

A Temple From Earliest Times

The dry climate of Southern Upper Egypt is perfect for preserving ancient remains and preventing decay. Experts therefore know more about ancient southern Egypt than about the north, where the land is more marshy, making both excavation and preservation difficult.

The first four nomes of Upper Egypt were important in Predynastic times. Hierakonpolis (now known as Kom el-Ahmar) was one of the earliest towns to be built along the Nile. The Predynastic settlement was a lively city that extended more than 5 kilometres (3 miles) along the edge of the Western Desert.

In the First Dynasty, a new town and temple were built on the flood plain. The temple is the oldest in Egypt that historians know about in detail. Treasures found in the temple include mace heads and palettes. They are the only record of some of the early Egyptian rulers. There were also ivory figurines, a golden hawk and life-size copper statues of two Sixth Dynasty kings.

This ancient relief of deities and a ruler is on the wall of the Greco-Roman temple overlooking the River Nile at Kom Ombo. Half of the temple was dedicated to Sobek, the crocodile god, and the other half to Haroeris, who was a form of the falcon god Horus. Sacred crocodiles were reared in a pool inside the temple grounds. There was also a cemetery for mummified crocodiles.

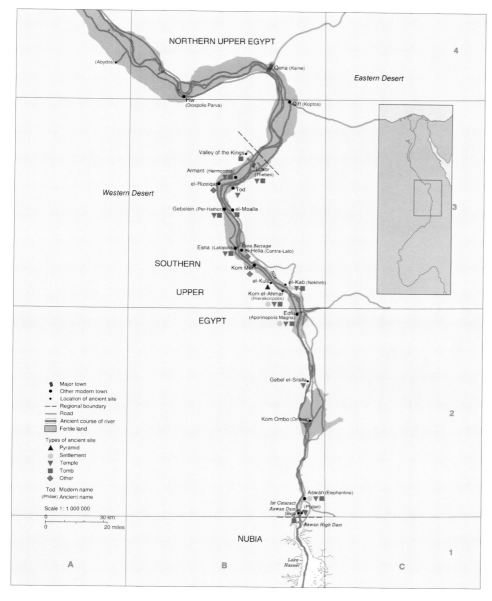

NORTHERN UPPER EGYPT

(Abydos)

Qena (Kaine)

Eastern Desert

Hiw
(Diospolis Parva)

Qift (Koptos)

Valley of the Kings

Armant (Hermonthis)

Luxor
(Thebes)

el-Rizeiqat

Tod

Western Desert

Gebelein (Per-Hathor)

el-Moalla

Esna (Latopolis)

Esna Barrage
el-Hella (Contra-Lato)

SOUTHERN

Kom Mer

UPPER

el-Kula

el-Kab (Nekheb)

Kom el-Ahmar
(Hierakonpolis)

EGYPT

Edfu
(Apollinopolis Magna)

Gebel el-Silsila

Kom Ombo (Ombos)

Major town
Other modern town
Location of ancient site
Regional boundary
Road
Ancient course of river
Fertile land

Types of ancient site
▲ Pyramid
● Settlement
▼ Temple
■ Tomb
◆ Other

Tod Modern name
(Philae) Ancient name

Scale 1 : 1 000 000

0   30 km
0   20 miles

Nile

Aswan (Elephantine)

1st Cataract
Aswan Dam

(Philae)
(Biga)

Aswan High Dam

NUBIA

Lake
Nasser

4

3

2

1

A

B

C

This map shows the most important historic centres of Southern Upper Egypt. The leading archaeological sites – Aswan, Philae, Biga, Edfu and Thebes – are described in more detail on the following pages.

people were cut into the desert cliffs.

Every large town in ancient Egypt contained a necropolis, or 'city of the dead'. Its streets were lined with tombs instead of houses. The desert necropolises often survived long after towns on the flood plain disappeared.

Greco–Roman Temples

The most spectacular remains in Southern Upper Egypt consist of a series of impressive temples dating back to the Greco–Roman period late in Egyptian history. There are examples at Philae, Aswan, Kom Ombo, Edfu, el-Kab, Esna and Tod. Although the temples were built when the country was under foreign rule, they are traditionally Egyptian in style.

Edfu is the most famous and probably the best preserved of all the temples, but the temples at Esna and Kom Ombo are also outstanding examples of temple architecture. Esna was dedicated to the ram god Khnum. A calendar inscribed on the walls tells us about the many festivals that were celebrated there. The temple at Kom Ombo is unusual because the left side of the structure is dedicated to one deity (the falcon god Haroeris, also known as Horus the Elder), and the right side to another, the crocodile god Sobek.

An Ancient Town

Nekheb (modern-day el-Kab) is another important site dating from Predynastic times. This settlement developed into a typical Egyptian town. The houses were built close together inside a huge mud-brick enclosure wall. The main temple, dedicated to the local vulture goddess, was situated inside the town. It was rebuilt many times over a period of about 3,000 years. Smaller temples were built on the edge of the desert, while the tombs of important

City of Aswan

Aswan took its ancient name of Elephantine from the elephant-ivory trade. The main part of the city was situated on Elephantine Island in the middle of the Nile River.

Aswan was close to the border between Egypt and Nubia. Troops were stationed there to protect the border and to take part in mining and trading expeditions. All the gold from the Nubian mines passed through Aswan. Donkey trains took desert routes to trade with African peoples.

In a Sixth-Dynasty tomb at Aswan there is an account of some trading trips. The tomb owner was a courtier named Harkhuf. He tells how his explorations took him south. Each trip took seven or eight months. On the third trip he returned

Reliefs at the temple of Edfu tell the story of how Horus, the hawk-headed god, defeated the god Seth.

home with 300 donkeys carrying precious goods such as ivory, ebony, incense, and leopard skins.

Best of all, he had brought back a pygmy to dance for the king. Harkhuf quotes a letter from King Pepy II. The king, who was a young boy, was thrilled. He ordered Harkhuf to hurry to the palace by boat. The pygmy was to be guarded day and night. "Check on him 10 times a night!" wrote Pepy. "My Majesty wants to see this pygmy more than all the treasures of Sinai and Punt!"

Holy Islands

Philae and Biga are a pair of islands in the Nile River just below Aswan. On Biga Island was the Abaton, a mound that was linked with the god Osiris.

When Set murdered Osiris he tore the body into many pieces. Biga was said to be the place where the left leg of Osiris was buried. In one version of the myth Isis, the wife of Osiris, collected the pieces and joined them by magic. Several places claimed to be the site where the whole body of Osiris was buried. Biga was one. The soul of Osiris was thought to haunt the island in the form of a bird. Biga was so holy that only priests could land there.

Philae was sacred to Isis. The temple of Isis was the largest of several temples and shrines on the island. Most of the buildings date to Greco-

Roman times. Pilgrims came from all over the Roman Empire to worship Isis here.

The last known inscriptions in ancient Egyptian are at Philae. The religion of Egypt survived here for longer than in any other place.

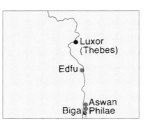

Many of the buildings were in excellent condition until building of the first Aswan Dam began in 1898. Once the dam was finished, Philae and Biga were flooded for most of each year. When the second Aswan Dam was constructed they were permanently submerged. The temples of Philae were reassembled on Agilika Island about 550 metres (600 yd) from their original site and are now well above the water level again.

Temple at Edfu

There was a walled town at Edfu from the Old Kingdom onwards. The site was ideal for settlement because it was near the the river but on high ground that was safe from flooding. Walls surround the site of the city, most of which has not been excavated.

The site is now famous for its Temple of Horus. Few buildings from the ancient world are as well preserved as this temple. It was almost completely intact when it was first excavated in the 1860s. Inscriptions give many construction details. It was begun under Ptolemy III in 237 BCE and took about 180 years to complete. The massive pillars of the hypostyle (Greek for 'bearing pillars') hall were designed to imitate a thicket of marsh plants. On some pillars the figures of the Egyptian gods were damaged by early Christian visitors and have been almost erased. Within the temple, the pillars add to a subtle pattern of light and darkness. Some rooms are entirely dark; others are lit by shafts of light that shine between the pillars.

On the great pylon (gateway) Ptolemy XII strikes a group of prisoners with a mace. Egyptian kings had been shown in this pose for nearly 3,000 years. Inside the temple are reliefs depicting Horus fighting the enemies of his father, Osiris. The evil god Set turns himself into a hippopotamus, but Horus fearlessly hunts him down with a magical harpoon. This story was acted out each year during the festival of The Victory of Horus. Inside the pylon is a large temple courtyard, which is the only one preserved in Egypt. The decorated walls of the courtyard continue to form an enclosure behind the temple.

A colonnade leads to the pylon, or gateway, of the reconstructed temple of Isis at Philae. The colonnades that welcomed pilgrims and led them towards the sanctuary were probably later additions to the temple. The first structures on the island were built during the 2th Dynasty, in the seventh century BCE.

Thebes

During the period
of the Old Kingdom, Thebes was little more than a small provincial town. When a local dynasty reunited Egypt following the First

Intermediate Period, however, Thebes soon grew to become an important administrative and religious centre. From the New Kingdom onwards, it was one of the largest urban areas in all of Egypt. Its magnificent buildings were famous throughout the ancient world. Thebes is actually a Greek name; the Egyptians called the city Waset.

Thebes covered an area of about 8 square kilometres (3 sq. mi) and was located on both sides of the River Nile. The east bank was reserved for the living, while the west bank was mainly a necropolis for the dead. Today, the site

Floodlights illuminate the forecourt of Amenophis III in the temple at Luxor. Amenophis was largely responsible for building the inner part of the temple. The forecourt leads to a series of antechambers, including a shrine celebrating the king's birth.

of Eastern Thebes is largely covered by the modern city of Luxor. Little remains of the ancient houses and splendid palaces that once stood on the site, although some of the great stone temples have survived.

City of the Dead
A mountain, known as 'The Peak', loomed over Western Thebes. The Egyptians believed the mountain was an entrance to the Underworld where people went after death. They therefore positioned as many of the royal tombs as close to the foot of the mountain as possible. The tombs were cut into the cliffs and ravines close to the Peak. The necropolis was known as 'The Place of Truth'.

The builders, artists and sculptors who constructed, decorated and maintained the royal tombs lived in a settlement at Deir el-Medina in housing provided by the government. Their homes, shrines and family tombs have been well preserved and extensively excavated. Today we know more about these people than about any other ancient Egyptian community.

The Valley of the Kings

The pyramid burials of Old and Middle Kingdom rulers were soon robbed of their treasures. From the 18th Dynasty onwards, the rulers tried instead to hide their burial places. Enene, the chief architect of Amonhotep I and Thutmose I, tells us: 'I oversaw the cutting out of the rock tomb of his Majesty in a lonely place where nobody could look on.' This lonely place was the Valley of the Kings, located in Western Thebes.

Throughout the New Kingdom, rulers were buried in tombs hidden in the valley. Mortuary temples were built on the west bank to serve the cult of the dead kings. Some rulers also built palaces in Western Thebes. The largest was the palace of Amonhotep III at Malqata.

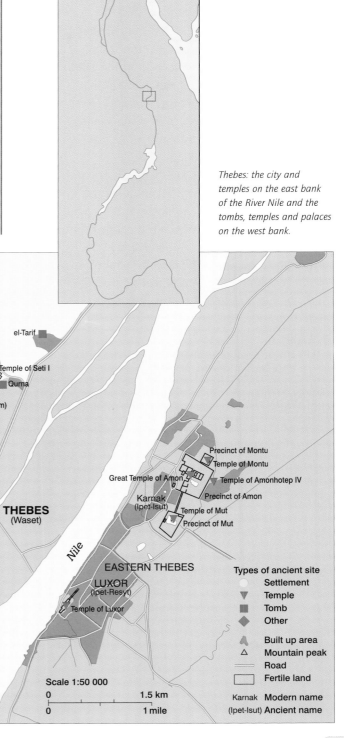

Thebes: the city and temples on the east bank of the River Nile and the tombs, temples and palaces on the west bank.

Tomb of Sons of Ramesses II

West Valley

VALLEY OF THE KINGS

Tomb of Amonhotep III

Tomb of Aya

East Valley

Tomb of Horemheb

Tomb of Tutankhamon

DEIR EL-BAHRI

Temple of Hatshepsut

el-Tarif

Temple of Amon

Temple of Mentuhotep

el-Qurn (The Peak) △

(The Place of Truth)

Asasif

Dra Abu el-Naga

Temple of Seti I

Tomb of Hatshepsut

Sheikh Abd el-Qurna

Temple of Ramesses IV

Qurna

DEIR EL-MEDINA

Tomb of Pashed

Temple of Hathor

Temple of Thutmose III

VALLEY OF THE QUEENS

Craftsmen's Village

Temple of Ramesses II (Ramesseum)

Tombs of the Queens

Temple of Thutmose IV

WESTERN THEBES

Temple of Merneptah

Temple of Aya and Horemheb

Site of Temple of Amonhotep III

Temple and Palace of Ramesses III

Colossi of Memnon

MEDINET HABU

Temple of Thoth

MALQATA

Palace of Amonhotep III

Precinct of Montu

Temple of Montu

Great Temple of Amon

Temple of Amonhotep IV

Karnak (Ipet-Isut)

Precinct of Amon

Temple of Mut

Precinct of Mut

THEBES (Waset)

Birket Habu

EASTERN THEBES

LUXOR (Ipet-Resyt)

Temple of Luxor

Nile

Temple of Isis

Types of ancient site

- ○ Settlement
- ▽ Temple
- ■ Tomb
- ◆ Other

Built up area

△ Mountain peak

Road

▭ Fertile land

Karnak   Modern name

(Ipet-Isut) Ancient name

Scale 1:50 000

0   1.5 km

0   1 mile

Luxor

The god Amon was the local deity of Thebes. After the ruler of Thebes had expelled the Hyskos from Egypt and founded the 18th Dynasty, Amon became an important fertility god throughout Egypt.

The god had two main temples in Thebes: Karnak in the north, and Luxor in the south. Most of the Luxor temple was built in the 18th Dynasty during the reign of Amonhotep III. Ramesses II later added a courtyard and pylon, or a gateway supported on pillars. The avenue of sphinxes that joined Luxor to Karnak was added during the Late Period.

The Luxor temple has one of the most impressive entrances of any Egyptian temple. The pylon has carvings that illustrate Ramsesses II's bravery at the battle of Qadesh against the Hittites. Outside the pylon stand some huge statues of Ramesses II. The temple is built around two courtyards. A narrow colonnade, which formed a route for processions, links them. The walls were decorated with scenes from the Festival of Opet, one of the most important of all the festivals held in Thebes.

During the annual festival, the Amon of Karnak visited Luxor for 11 days. The cult statues of Amon, his wife Mut and their sons Khons were placed in beautiful decorated boats on the Nile. Watched by huge crowds, the vessels were towed from Karnak to Luxor. Acrobats, dancers and musicians formed a procession on the river bank.

New Uses for Ancient Temples

Deep inside the temple is a room decorated with reliefs that tell the story of the birth of Amonhotep III. Close to this room is an area of the temple that was turned into a shrine to the Roman emperors in around 300 CE. Nearly 1,000 years later a mosque (Muslim place of worship) was built in the courtyard of Ramesses II. The mosque is still in use today.

Karnak

Karnak is the site of a group of temples that cover an area of about 1.6 square kilometres (1 sq. mi). The most important temple was the Great Temple of Amon. The name Amon means 'the hidden one'. He was the god of invisible forces like the wind. He became an important god during the Middle Kingdom. Few

Most pillars in the Great Hypostyle Hall at Karnak, built in the 13th century BCE, fell down during earthquakes but were reconstructed in the 19th century.

Middle Kingdom temples survive because each pharaoh wanted to please Amon by building a new temple to him. They knocked down existing temples and reused the stones. The Great Temple was continually enlarged and rebuilt over a period of 2,000 years.

The Triumph of Amon

In the early 18th Dynasty, Thebes became the capital of Egypt. Amon was linked with the sun god, Ra, and the new deity Amon-Ra was credited with creating the world.

During the New Kingdom, Karnak became the largest and richest temple complex in Egypt. The complex included a sacred lake, smaller temples and shrines surrounded by a mud-brick enclosure. The eastern part is the oldest. Successive kings built new entrances so the temple now has ten huge pylons (gateways).

The most famous part of the temple is the Great Hypostyle Hall. Begun by Seti I and finished by Ramesses II, the huge hall has 134 columns. In one of its many courtyards 751 stone statues and stelae and 17,000 bronze figurines were found buried.

City of the Dead

The other main buildings at Karnak include temples to the god Montu and the creator god Ptah. The temple of Mut once held more than 700 granite statues.

Thebes West Bank Sites

After King Mentuhotep reunited Egypt in 2040 BCE, he built himself a tomb and temple on the west bank at Deir el-Bahri. Nearly 600 years later, Queen Hatshepsut built her temple against the cliff face of Deir el-Bahri. Other pharaohs also built here, including Ramesses II. His temple is called the Ramesseum and was the site of the first strike over wages, in 1165 BCE, by necropolis workers.

A town grew up around the great temple of Ramesses III at Medinet Habu, the best-preserved mortuary temple of Thebes. Its strong fortifications meant that Medinet Habu was used as a safe place in times of unrest.

The funeral procession of Tutankhamon. The royal coffins lie on a frame inside a bark (boat) shrine. The shrine, mounted on a sled, is dragged along by courtiers and a team of oxen. The courtiers wear white headbands, a sign of mourning. Next comes an alabaster shrine shouldered by priests. This holds the four canopic jars containing the liver, lungs, stomach and intestines of the king.

All kinds of people were buried in the Theban necropolis. One 11th Dynasty tomb held the bodies of 60 soldiers killed in battle. Paintings in royal tombs usually showed traditional rituals while the art in private tombs showed everyday life. The Tombs of the Nobles were for those of high office. Many contain magnificent paintings and some remained unfinished because their owners suddenly fell from royal favour.

Members of the royal families were buried in the Valley of the Queens. The finest tomb there belonged to Queen Nefertari.

The Royal Mummies

Sixty-three tombs have been found in the Valley of the Kings. In most, rock-cut passages and stairways lead to the burial chamber. The walls are decorated with religious scenes. Seti I and Ramesses VI had the most elaborate tombs.

Each king was buried with valuable funerary objects. By the end of the New Kingdom, most of the tombs had been robbed. Under the 21st Dynasty, many of the royal mummies were moved to a secret hiding place where they remained hidden until 1881. Now the rulers rest in the Egyptian Museum in Cairo.

NORTHERN UPPER EGYPT

Northern Upper Egypt was the heartland of ancient Egypt. It was where the ancient Egyptian civilisation first emerged. The Badarian/Tasian and Naqada cultures, the early predecessors from whom the Egyptians developed, are named after sites in this region that have yielded evidence of early settlement. The discovery of easily mined gold in the Eastern Desert was a key factor in the rise of an early kingdom centred on Northern Upper Egypt. Just as important as the presence of gold were the trade routes that led east from this part of the Nile across the desert to the Red Sea and the shipping routes that began there. The major route was the Wadi Hammamat, which ran along a dry river bed.

Gold mines and stone quarries lay along the wadi. Ship parts and cargo boxes dating back over 4,000 years have recently been found in caves on the Red Sea coast. The physical evidence confirmed what archaeologists studying ancient trade have long thought. Ships that carried goods on the Nile were dismantled and carried through the wadi on the 160-kilometre (100-mi) journey to the Red Sea. At the coast, the ships were put back together for the journey north to carry turquoise miners to Sinai or south to Yemen or Punt (possibly modern-day Eritrea) to trade for spices and incense. On the return journey, the ships were taken apart again to be carried back to the Nile.

A Holy Place

Another site in northern Upper Egypt that started to be important in early times was Abydos. It was a religious rather than a political centre. Some of the predynastic and first and second Dynasty kings were buried in tombs close to Abydos. The city's main god was Khentanetiu (Chief of the Westerners). The Westerners were the spirits of the dead who had reached the Egyptian paradise – 'the beautiful West'. From the late Old Kingdom, Khentamentiu was linked to the god Osiris.

During the Middle and New Kingdoms, Abydos was the most important of a number of places that claimed to be the burial site of Osiris. Every year, a festival was held there that told the story of Osiris's murder and rebirth. Pilgrims came from all over Egypt to attend, and every Egyptian wanted to visit Abydos at least once in their life. The festival was a favourite subject in tomb paintings, so that a person who had not managed to make the journey in life would be able to make it after death.

Another belief was that by building a tomb or monument at Abydos a person could share in the resurrection of Osiris. Not only kings but also ordinary Egyptians put up stelae (carved pillars) so their spirits could join Osiris.

The Shadow of Thebes

From the Middle Kingdom onwards, the town of Thebes grew rapidly, overshadowing all the other towns of Northern Upper Egypt. New Kingdom rulers did build temples at Abydos, Koptos and Dendara, but they were far outshone by the size and wealth of the temples at Thebes. Thebes remained the most important political and religious centre in the region until the end of the Late Period.

Under Greek and Roman rule other towns flourished. During the Greco–Roman period, many fine temples were built at sites like Dendara, Nag el-Madamud, Akhmim and Hiw. These temples usually replaced earlier, simpler buildings. The god Min was worshipped at Koptos for 3,500 years, and his temple was rebuilt many times during that period. Among the objects found in this temple were three huge statues of Min. They are the oldest colossal stone statues in the world.

Northern Upper Egypt was the heartland of Egypt's earliest dynasties, which had political and religious centres at Naqada, Qift and Abydos. During the Old Kingdom, Dendara was important. The Middle Kingdom was dominated by Abydos, while the New Kingdom saw the rise of Thebes. Dendara and Abydos are described in more detail on the following pages.

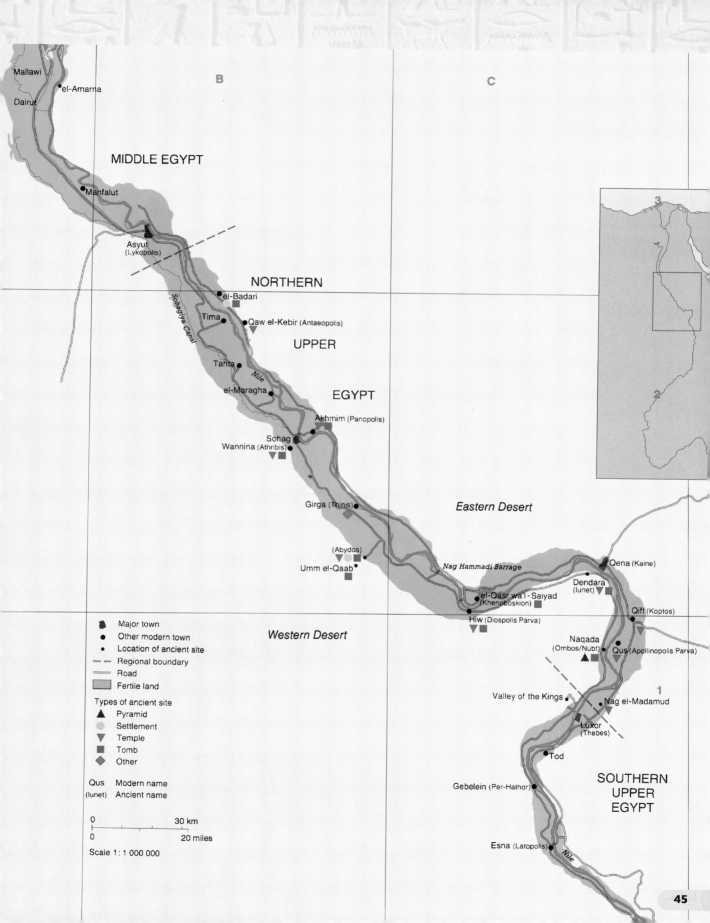

Mallawi
el-Amarna
Dairut

MIDDLE EGYPT

Manfalut

Asyut
(Lykopolis)

NORTHERN

Sohagiya Canal

el-Badari

Tima

Qaw el-Kebir (Antaeopolis)

UPPER

Tahta

Nile

el-Maragha

EGYPT

Akhmim (Panopolis)

Sohag
Wannina (Athribis)

Girga (Thinis)

Eastern Desert

(Abydos)

Umm el-Qaab

Nag Hammadi Barrage

Qena (Kaine)

Dendara
(Iunet)

el-Qasr wa'l-Saiyad
(Khenoboskion)

Qift (Koptos)

Hiw (Diospolis Parva)

Western Desert

Naqada
(Ombos/Nubt)

Qus (Apollinopolis Parva)

Valley of the Kings

Nag el-Madamud

Luxor
(Thebes)

Tod

SOUTHERN
UPPER
EGYPT

Gebelein (Per-Hathor)

Esna (Latopolis)

Nile

🏛	Major town
●	Other modern town
•	Location of ancient site
– – –	Regional boundary
═══	Road
▨	Fertile land

Types of ancient site

▲ Pyramid
⬤ Settlement
▽ Temple
◼ Tomb
◆ Other

Qus Modern name
(Iunet) Ancient name

0 _____ 30 km
0 _____ 20 miles

Scale 1 : 1 000 000

B

C

3

1

2

45

Dendara

During the Old Kingdom and the First Intermediate Period, Dendara was a very important town in Northern Upper Egypt. It was the capital of the 6th nome of Upper Egypt, but its main importance was due to its religious connections. It was the main cult centre of Hathor, who was a popular goddess of birth and death. Hathor was originally worshipped as a personification of the Milky Way and later as a cow-deity whose milk helped nourish humankind. Various cow burials have been found in the necropolis. The goddess was also connected with love, music, foreign lands and precious metals.

Every year, the cult statue of Hathor made a ritual journey from Dendara to Edfu for the festival of her 'marriage' to the god Horus, who later became associated with the sun-god Ra. Horus and the couple's son, Ihy, each had their own temple at Dendara. Today, only the temple complex of Hathor still stands.

The Sacred Area

A sacred lake lay inside the enclosure wall of the Hathor temple. Priests washed in the lake to purify themselves before entering a sanctuary. Among the buildings near the temple are a sanatorium (hospital) and two 'birth houses'. Sick people slept in the sanitorium in the hope that Hathor would tell them in a dream how to cure their sickness. Patients also drank or bathed in sacred water to heal themselves.

A birth house was a special shrine that celebrated the birth of a deity or god. At Dendara, reliefs in the two birth houses show Hathor giving birth to her son Ihy. Pregnant Egyptian women prayed to Hathor, Lady of Dendara, to bring them safely through the process of giving birth.

The Temple of Hathor

The temple of Hathor at Dendara was built and decorated between the second century BCE and the first century CE. It was the largest and most elaborately decorated temple built anywhere in Egypt during the period. Among its most notable features are two wonderful columned halls. At the top of the columns were capitals which took the shape of a sistrum, a musical instrument sacred to the goddess. Several shrines were also built on top of the flat roof. Two were dedicated to the god Osiris. They were reached by staircases that were built inside the temple walls. The roof is quite rare among Egyptian ruins. Very few ceiling structures survive in ancient Egyptian temples.

Sacred treasures were once hidden in small underground rooms near the sanctuary. On the back wall of the temple, Cleopatra VII appears with her son by Julius Caesar. In the middle of this wall is a huge symbol of Hathor. Most visitors prayed to the goddess at this spot.

Abydos

Excavations in the southern part of Abydos have revealed the presence of a Middle Kingdom and Second Intermediate Period town. Little of the main temple of Osiris, located in central Abydos, remains. The necropolis (city of the dead) of Abydos spreads along the desert edge for about 1.6 kilometres (1 mi). The first burials were made there in the fourth millennium BCE.

The Mother of Pots

The earliest royal tombs at Abydos were underground palaces with brick-lined rooms. They are near the area known as Umm el-Qaab (which means 'Mother of Pots') and date to the little-known Dynasty O. Some First-Dynasty kings built tombs at Umm el-Qaab and huge brick enclosures nearer to the town. The tomb of King Djer was later mistaken for the tomb of Osiris.

Umm el-Qaab gets its name from the thousands of pieces of pottery left by pilgrims in what they thought was Osiris' tomb.

The Temple of Seti I

Several kings built mortuary temples in the southern part of Abydos. The best preserved of these is the temple of King Seti I. Known as the Memnonium, it was built of fine white limestone. Originally, there were two pylons, two courtyards and two columned halls. The plan of the inner area is unique. It has seven sanctuaries side by side.

One sanctuary was for the worship of the cult of Seti, and another was dedicated to Osiris. Its walls are decorated with scenes from the myth of Osiris. The reliefs are some of the most beautiful in all of Egyptian art. They show ceremonies associated with the gods. In another part of the temple, Seti is shown with his heir, Ramesses II, making offerings to royal ancestors. Ramesses completed his father's tomb and built his own nearby.

Behind Seti I's temple is a mysterious building known as the Osireion. It was probably started by Seti I and finished by his grandson, Merneptah. The main feature was an underground hall built in red granite. In the middle of the hall there was an artificial island and a canal was dug to surround the island with water. A sarcophagus was placed on the island. The building could have been a dummy royal tomb, a model of the tomb of Osiris or a re-creation of the first mound of land rising above the waters of chaos.

This painting from Abydos was created in about 1413 BCE, during the 18th Dynasty, to decorate the tomb of Sennefer, the mayor of Thebes. It shows oarsmen rowing a Nile boat under the watchful eye of an overseer. At the back of the vessel is the helmsman.

The term Middle Egypt describes an area of some 290 kilometres (180 mi) of the Nile Valley from Asyut in the south to Memphis in the north. Asyut was the most southern part of the Herakleopolitan kingdom during the First Intermediate Period. It lay near the traditional boundary between the southern and northern administrative areas of Upper Egypt. Middle Egypt also includes the Faiyum, a large area of fertile land jutting out into the Western Desert. A branch of the River Nile flowed through the Faiyum into Lake Moeris. This lake was much bigger in ancient times than it is today. The Faiyum became an important area during the Middle Kingdom and retained its importance for the rest of the ancient period.

During the Third Intermediate and Late Periods Middle Egypt benefited from its position at the meeting point between the delta and the south. In late antiquity it prospered as a commercial centre, trading with the oases in the desert.

Royal Tombs and Cities

Although there are relatively few large temples in Middle Egypt, there are a lot of interesting tombs. Some kings were buried in this area during the late Old Kingdom and the first Intermediate Period in tombs dug into cliffs at the edge of the desert plateau. There is a Third/Fourth Dynasty royal pyramid at Maidum, and Middle Kingdom rulers built pyramids at el-Lisht, el-Lahun and Hawara.

These 12th-Dynasty pyramids were generally poorly constructed and are now in ruins. The huge mortuary temple of Amenemhet III at Hawara was famous throughout the ancient world as 'The Labyrinth'. Almost nothing of it survives today. No trace has been found of the 12th-Dynasty capital, Itjtawy, which lay somewhere near el-Lisht. In the 18th Dynasty, another capital city and royal necropolis was built in Middle Egypt at el-Amarna. It was only the royal residence for a few years, however, as part of an Egyptian king's attempt to reform Egyptian religion. The religious reforms did not outlast their creator. The pharaoh's name was scratched off the stone monuments and his capital city was abandoned only 15 years after it was built. The brief period of occupation means that the city is of great interest to archaeologists. Although few ruins stand today, experts have been able to excavate traces of the town plan, which was not obscured by later building and rebuilding.

The Nomarchs of Middle Egypt

Form the Sixth Dynasty to the late 12th Dynasty, the nomarchs of Middle Egypt enjoyed much power and independence. They built themselves magnificent rock-cut tombs along the edges of the desert and were buried in coffins painted with maps that would help their souls find the way through the Underworld after death. The nomarchs of Herakleopolis called themselves kings in the First Intermediate Period.

Herakleopolis and Hermopolis were both the capital towns of some minor kings during the Third Intermediate Period. Hermopolis, which the Egyptians called the City of the Eight (meaning eight gods), was located on the west bank of the River Nile, between Thebes and Memphis. It was the main centre of the god, Thoth, the god of the moon, wisdom and writing. A huge temple complex once stood here. The monuments that survive include two huge statues of Thoth as a baboon. Sacred baboons and ibises, the bird of Thoth, were buried in underground galleries in the necropolis at Tuna el-Gebel. There were painted tombs from the Greco–Roman period in the necropolis.

Middle Egypt was the northern part of what was traditionally called Upper Egypt and comprised the length of the Nile from Asyut in the south to Memphis in the north. Some of the major sites – Meir, Maidum, Beni Hasan and Akhenaten's short-lived capital at el-Amarna – are described in more detail on the following pages.

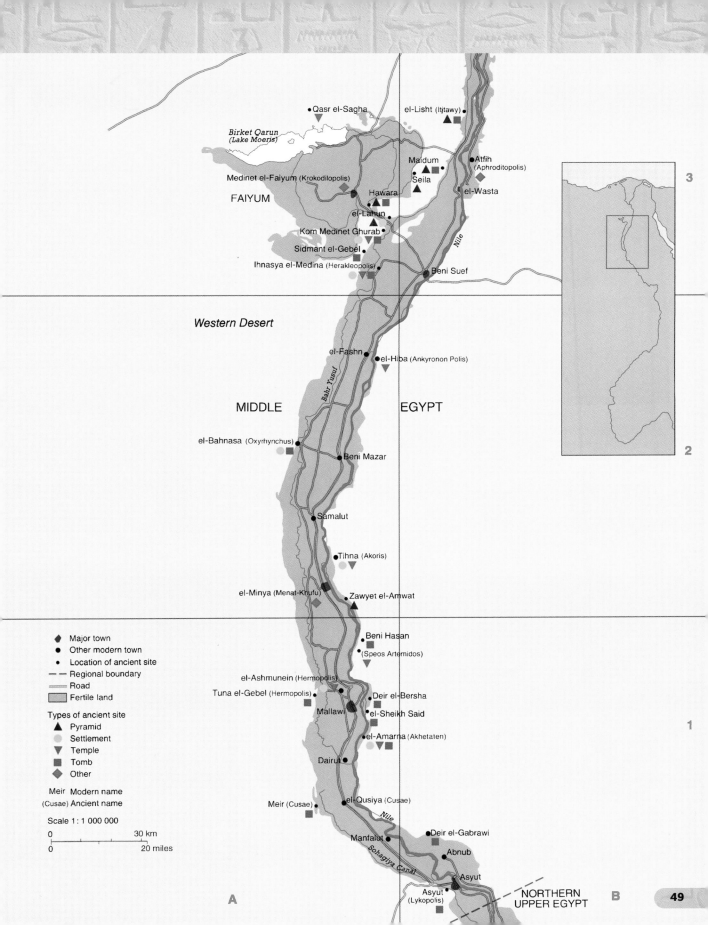

Qasr el-Sagha
el-Lisht (Itjtawy)
Birket Qarun (Lake Moeris)
Maidum
Atfih (Aphroditopolis)
Medinet el-Faiyum (Krokodilopolis)
Seila
FAIYUM
Hawara
el-Wasta
el-Lahun
Kom Medinet Ghurab
Sidmant el-Gebel
Ihnasya el-Medina (Herakleopolis)
Beni Suef

Western Desert

el-Fashn
el-Hiba (Ankyronon Polis)

MIDDLE   EGYPT

el-Bahnasa (Oxyrhynchus)
Beni Mazar

Samalut

Tihna (Akoris)

el-Minya (Menat-Khufu)
Zawyet el-Amwat

Beni Hasan
(Speos Artemidos)

el-Ashmunein (Hermopolis)
Tuna el-Gebel (Hermopolis)
Deir el-Bersha
Mallawi
el-Sheikh Said
el-Amarna (Akhetaten)
Dairut

Meir (Cusae)
el-Qusiya (Cusae)

Deir el-Gabrawi
Manfalut
Abnub
Sohagiya Canal
Asyut
Asyut (Lykopolis)
NORTHERN UPPER EGYPT

Bahr Yusuf
Nile

3
2
1

Legend

◆ Major town
● Other modern town
• Location of ancient site
- - Regional boundary
═══ Road
▒ Fertile land

Types of ancient site
▲ Pyramid
○ Settlement
▽ Temple
■ Tomb
◆ Other

Meir Modern name
(Cusae) Ancient name

Scale 1 : 1 000 000

0 ——————— 30 km
0 ——————— 20 miles

A   B

Meir

Traditional feluccas sail near the town of Asyut. With their distinctive triangular sails, which make them easier to sail into the wind, feluccas have been used to carry passengers and cargo on the Nile for thousands of years.

Meir is the site of the necropolis for the ancient town of Cusae, of which there are no remains. The town, which is located about 50 kilometres (30 mi) north-west of Asyut, was the administrative centre of a nome. The rock-cut tombs at Meir belong to the nomarchs of the Sixth and 12th Dynasties.

Each tomb comprised a large room cut directly into the cliff face. There are niches for statues and offerings and deep shafts for the coffins. The walls are decorated with painted reliefs. Common pictures include hunting in the desert and fishing in the marshes. Other images include vase-making and harvesting.

A festival, associated with Hathor, is depicted in several of the tombs. The late 12th Dynasty tomb of Wekh-hotep has some of the most delicate paintings that survive from the Middle Kingdom. They show the nomarch spearing fish and throwing a boomerang at marsh birds.

Maidum

Maidum is the site of a mysterious building disaster. All that remains of an early attempt to build a true pyramid – rather than a step-pyramid – is a strange-looking tower that rises out of a mound of rubble. The pyramid was the earliest to be built with a related pyramid complex. The original size of the pyramid itself was 144 metres (472 ft) square and 42 metres (138 ft) tall. It was probably begun for Huni, who was the last king of the Third Dynasty, but according to graffiti created in the New Kingdom, it may have been completed by his successor Snofru.

The Maidum pyramid was first created as a seven-stepped structure. Then an eighth step was built. The steps were filled in and a limestone casing was added to create a smooth-sided pyramid. Unfortunately, the outer cladding was not applied properly. It did not bond to the sides of the existing structure and it had no proper foundations. As a result, the outer parts of the pyramid collapsed. We do not know whether this happened just after the pyramid was finished or hundreds of years later; it may have been the latter, as a necropolis of early Fourth Dynasty mastaba (flat-roofed tombs) grew up nearby, which would be unlikely if the pyramid had already collapsed.

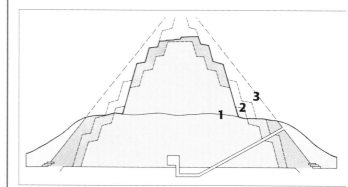

A section showing the three stages of the Maidum pyramid:
1 Seven-stepped pyramid.
2 Eight-stepped pyramid.
3 True geometric pyramid.

Beni Hasan

Decorated rock-cut

tombs belonging to Middle Egyptian nomarchs survive at sites at Asyut, Deir el-Gabrawi, Meir, el-Sheikh Said and Deir el-Bersha. The most interesting are the group found at Beni Hasan. There are 39 tombs here, dating from the 11th to the late 12th Dynasties. Wooden coffins, statuettes and models have been found in them. At least eight of the tombs belonged to the nomarchs of the Oryx nome. They were powerful in the region until the 12th Dynasty kings centralised power. The more elaborate tombs are made up of an outer court and portico and a rock-cut main room with elegant pillars. The walls were painted rather than carved. The ceilings, too, are painted.

They feature geometric patterns that imitate woven matting or textiles.

Scenes showing daily life cover most of the walls. Unusual paintings of battles and sieges illustrate wars between nomes. Other scenes show girls playing ball, men and baboons picking figs and the arrival of a group of traders from Palestine. The paintings became badly deteriorated but have since been restored.

In a nearby valley, almost 1.6 kilometres (1 mi) to the south of Beni Hasan, Queen Hatshepsut built a small temple. This unfinished rock-cut temple is known as Seos Artemidos and was dedicated to a lioness goddess called Pakhet. Her name means 'she who scratches'.

In inscriptions, the names of rulers were inscribed in lozenge-shaped features that Egyptologists call 'cartouches'. The cartouche contains a series of hieroglyphs that give the king's name and describe the qualities associated with him.

El Amarna

One of the great cities of ancient Egypt was el-Amarna in Middle Egypt. Its power only lasted for about 15 years. Its Egyptian name was Akhetaten, which means 'The Horizon of the Sun Disk'. When the pharaoh Akhenaten decided to build a new capital to complement the new religion he had founded, dedicated to the sun god Aten, he chose a site on a flat stretch of land beside the Nile valley that had never been inhabited. About 1349 BCE, work

began, and the city soon spread rapidly to cover an area of about 5 square kilometres (2 sq. mi). The city's population was probably around 30,000 or more. Akhenaten lived there with his queen Nefertiti.

A reconstruction of the villa of a high official at el-Amarna. Such villas were like miniature farms. Fruit and vegetables were grown in the gardens. There were beehive-shaped grain bins (centre right), a cattle yard and stalls and stables for chariot horses. Each villa had a shrine for worship of the Aten and the royal family (bottom left).

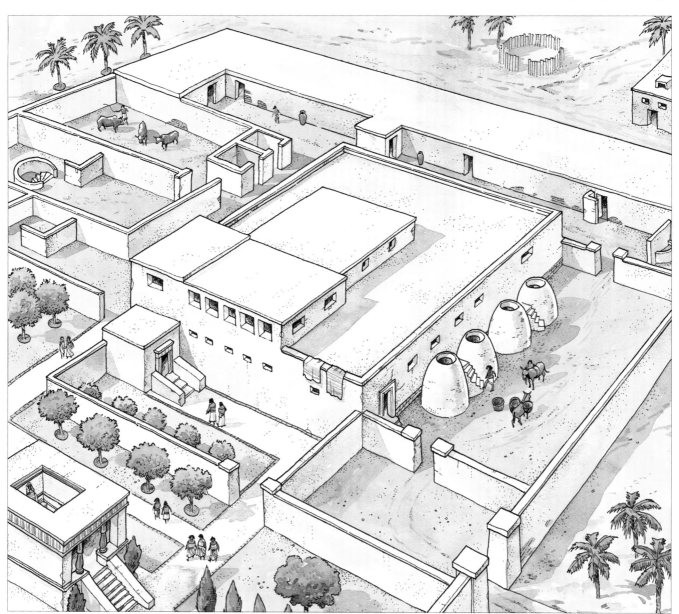

Palaces, Temples and Tombs

El-Amarna became the chief royal residence and the centre of government. There were at least five palaces, many official buildings and several necropolises, as well as a number of zoos and gardens. In the palaces, floors and ceilings were painted or tiled in brilliant colours. One room in the North Palace had a beautiful painting of birds in a papyrus thicket that covered three walls. Akhenaten's private apartments were decorated with charming pictures of Queen Nefertiti and the little princesses. Important officials, like the

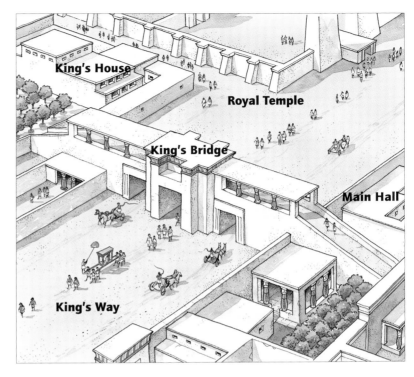

RIGHT: This picture shows part of the central city c.1340 BCE. The King's Way was 40 metres (130ft) wide. It passed under the King's Bridge, linking the Great Palace to Akhenaten's private apartments (the King's House). The Great Palace had a series of stone courts and halls. The Royal Temple, built for the Aten, was the second largest in the city.

BELOW: Plan of the areas of el-Amarna excavated so far. The temples and altars marked were all dedicated to the Sun Disk (Aten). The purpose of some buildings, such as the Maru Aten, is uncertain. The workmen's village continued to be lived in for some time after the main city was abandoned.

NORTH CITY
North Palace
Altars
House T.36.11
NORTH SUBURBS
North Tombs
Great Temple
Great Palace
Record Office
Royal Temple
MAIN CITY
EL-AMARNA (AKHETATEN)
Tomb of Amonhotep IV (Akhenaten)
Workmen's Village
Nile
River Temple
Royal Enclosure

Types of ancient site
● Settlement
▼ Temple
■ Tomb
◆ Other

Maru Aten
South Tombs ■

Fertile land
Excavated area

Scale 1 : 87 000
0   1 km
0   1 mile

vizier, also had magnificently decorated homes at el-Amarna. The only gods worshipped at el-Armarna were the Aten (the Sun Disk) and Akhenaten himself. A new type of temple was built for Aten. Unlike other temples, these temples had huge courtyards with hundreds of altars open to the sun.

Tombs were cut in the desert hills for the royal family and favoured courtiers, but most were never used. Their paintings show the official view of life in el-Amarna. In many scenes the rays of the Sun Disk end in hands holding out the symbol of life to Akhenaten.

The Deserted City

Akhenaten's new ideas were not popular. After his death, people called him 'The Great Criminal'. During Tutankhamon's reign the city was abandoned and never lived in again. Everything of value was taken away. Portraits of the disgraced royal family, including the famous head of Nefertiti, were left behind in a sculptor's workshop.

MEMPHIS

Memphis was the first capital of a united Egypt. Today little survives, but for three thousand years it was one of the country's greatest cities. Ancient Memphis is now buried under modern towns and silt from the Nile. Around the palm groves of the village of Mit Rahina are the remains of a few major buildings. A colossal statue of Ramesses II lies where it was found, but it is now surrounded by a museum.

Ptah, the creator god, was the main deity of Memphis. A small part of the temple complex dedicated to Ptah has so far been excavated. It was once one of the largest temples in Egypt. Among the kings to be crowned there was Alexander the Great. The remains of palaces built by 19th and 26th Dynasty kings have been found at Mit Rahina.

A Sacred Bull

A sacred bull, known as the Apis Bull, represented Ptah. To be considered sacred, the bull had to have a white triangle on a black forehead, a scarab shape under its tongue and a further 27 special marks. If it fulfilled these requirements, the bull lived in great luxury. Each year, it led a procession at the festival of 'The Running of the Apis Bull'. When the bull died, it was mummified and put in a stone sarcophagus.

From the rule of Ramesses II, bulls were buried in underground galleries at Saqqara, which was part of the necropolis of Memphis. Above these galleries was a temple, known as the Serapeum. From the third century BCE, the main god of the temple was Serapis, created from Greek and Egyptian gods.

Other animals were also buried at Saqqara, including cows, which had given birth to the Apis Bulls, as well as sacred dogs, cats and ibises. People believed that by paying for the mummification and burial of an animal they would please the gods. Archaeologists have found the mummified bodies of many sacred ibises. In ancient Egypt, the ibis was thought to be an incarnation of the god Thoth.

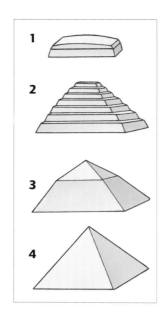

Tomb types in the Memphis necropolis:

1 Mastaba tomb, First–Sixth Dynasties.
2 Step pyramid, Third Dynasty.
3 Bent pyramid, Fourth Dynasty.
4 True pyramid, Old and Middle Kingdoms.

The Great Necropolis

The necropolis for the town of Memphis stretches for 30 kilometres (18 mi) along the edge of the Western Desert, between Dahshur and Abu Rawash. It is probably the largest cemetery in the world, as befits the status of Memphis. As well as the temples at Giza, there are around 50 smaller tombs. The royal tombs consist of step pyramids and true pyramids. From the Fourth Dynasty, each pyramid had two temples adjoining it – the valley temple and the mortuary temple.

The valley temple was located on the edge of the flood plain so it could be reached by boat. From the valley temple, the royal coffin was transported, via an enclosed causeway, to the mortuary temple. It was usually situated on the east side of the pyramid because the king hoped to be reborn like the rising sun. Priests made offerings to the king's spirit in the mortuary temple. This cult continued long after a king died. Towns were built to accommodate priests who continued to serve the dead king.

Smaller pyramids were also part of the pyramid complex. By the Middle Kingdom, royal ladies were buried in these pyramids. In the Old Kingdom, the smaller pyramids had been used to bury the king's vital organs. The mastaba tombs of high officials and lesser members of the royal family are organised around the Old Kingdom pyramids.

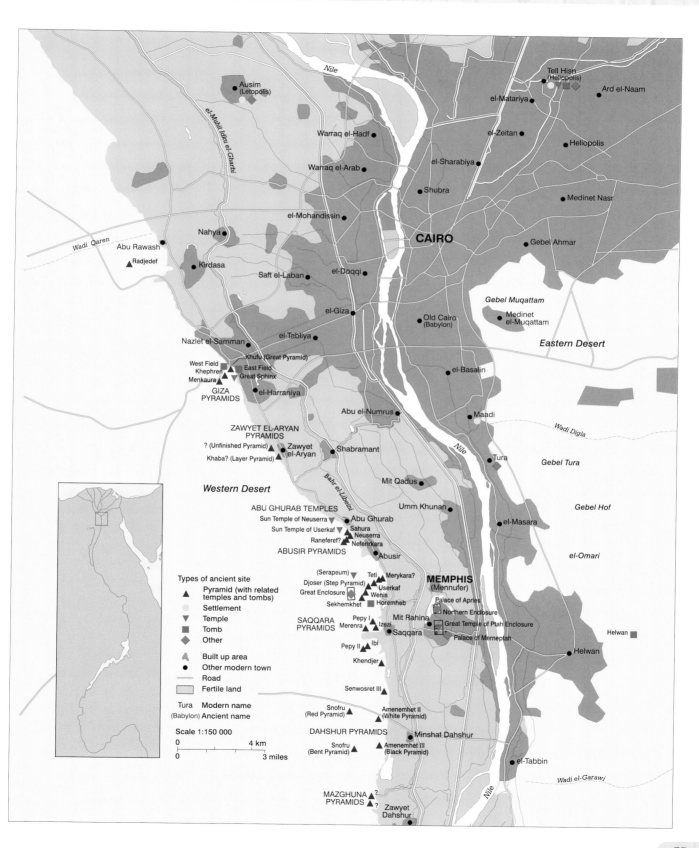

Nile

Ausim
(Letopolis)

el-Mahit Idku el-Gharbi

Tell Hisn
(Heliopolis)
Ard el-Naam

el-Matariya

Warraq el-Hadf

el-Zeitan

Heliopolis

Warraq el-Arab

el-Sharabiya

Shubra

el-Mohandissin

CAIRO

Medinet Nasr

Wadi Qaren

Nahya

Gebel Ahmar

Abu Rawash

Radjedef

Kirdasa

Saft el-Laban

el-Doqqi

el-Giza

Old Cairo
(Babylon)

Gebel Muqattam

Medinet
el-Muqattam

Eastern Desert

el-Tabliya

Nazlet el-Samman

Khufu (Great Pyramid)

West Field
Khephren   East Field
Menkaura   Great Sphinx

GIZA
PYRAMIDS

el-Harraniya

el-Basalin

Abu el-Numrus

Maadi

ZAWYET EL-ARYAN
PYRAMIDS

? (Unfinished Pyramid)

Zawyet
el-Aryan

Shabramant

Wadi Digla

Tura

Gebel Tura

Khaba? (Layer Pyramid)

Bahr el-Libeini

Mit Qadus

Western Desert

Gebel Hof

ABU GHURAB TEMPLES

Umm Khunan

Sun Temple of Neuserra

Abu Ghurab

el-Masara

Sun Temple of Userkaf

Sahura

Raneferef?

Neuserra

el-Omari

ABUSIR PYRAMIDS

Neferirkara

Abusir

(Serapeum)

Teti   Merykara?

MEMPHIS
(Mennufer)

Djoser (Step Pyramid)

Userkaf

Great Enclosure

Wenis

Palace of Apries

Sekhemkhet

Horemheb

Northern Enclosure

SAQQARA
PYRAMIDS

Pepy I

Mit Rahina

Great Temple of Ptah Enclosure

Merenra   Izezi

Saqqara

Helwan

Pepy II   Ibi

Palace of Merneptah

Khendjer

Helwan

Senwosret III

Snofru
(Red Pyramid)

Amenemhet II
(White Pyramid)

DAHSHUR PYRAMIDS

Minshat Dahshur

Snofru
(Bent Pyramid)

Amenemhet III
(Black Pyramid)

el-Tabbin

Wadi el-Garawi

MAZGHUNA
PYRAMIDS

?

?   Zawyet
Dahshur

Nile

Types of ancient site

▲ Pyramid (with related
   temples and tombs)

○ Settlement

▼ Temple

■ Tomb

◆ Other

▲ Built up area

● Other modern town

— Road

Fertile land

Tura   Modern name
(Babylon)   Ancient name

Scale 1:150 000

0   4 km

0   3 miles

55

Dahshur

Snofru, the first king of the Fourth Dynasty, built two stone pyramids at Dahshur, which is located in the southernmost part of the necropolis of Memphis.

The Bent Pyramid

This pyramid was most likely the first royal tomb to be designed as a true pyramid. When it was half finished, the angle of the outer surface was made smaller to give the sides a gentler slope. Also, a new way of laying the casing stones was used. The changes were probably made to stop the pyramid from collapsing like the one at Maidum. The Red Pyramid (named after the red limestone used to build it) is a huge true pyramid. It was built at the same angle as the upper part of the Bent Pyramid.

Royal Treasures

Three 12th Dynasty rulers – Amenemhet II, Senwosret III and Amenemhet III – each built mud-brick pyramids, finished in stone, at Dahshur. Two lesser 13th Dynasty kings were buried nearby. In a pit close to the pyramid of Senwosret III, archaeologists have found six wooden boats.

The tombs of the royal women were located around the 12th Dynasty pyramids. Wonderful jewellery made from gold and precious stones have been found at seven of the burial sites.

Saqqara

For more than three thousand years, Saqqara was an important cemetery. From as early as the Second Dynasty, kings were buried here. The most famous monument is the Step Pyramid. There are 13 other pyramids built between the Third and 13th Dynasties.

The Writing on the Walls

The pyramid of the last king of the Fifth Dynasty, Wenis, was the earliest to be inscribed with the Pyramid Texts, a series of magic spells, written in vertical columns in hieroglyphic script. The spells were to help the king become a god in the afterlife.

Reliefs decorate the causeway that connected the pyramid to the valley temple. They show workers bringing stone columns to Saqqara from Aswan, and workers collecting honey. There is also an inscription noting that a later pharaoh repaired the pyramid about 1,200 years after it was originally built.

Decorated Tombs

From the Early Dynastic times, high officials were buried in mastaba tombs at Saqqara. The best were built in the Fifth and Sixth Dynasties. The small rooms of the tombs were highly decorated to show the owner enjoying life. The mastaba of the vizier Mereruka was the biggest with 32 rooms. Its reliefs in the family tomb show scenes from daily life, including a hippopotamus hunt.

The next great period of tomb building at Saqqara was in the late 18th and early 19th Dynasties. High officials had rock-cut tombs or large stone tombs with pillared courts and chapels with miniature pyramids on top.

In the Late Period, tombs were made to be 'robber-proof'. Coffins were put in deep shafts and then covered with sand.

The huge step pyramid at Saqqara towers over a passing horse and rider. The pyramid was built for Djoser, a king of the Third Dynasty in the Old Kingdom, in about 2650 BCE. Its six steps were the forerunner of the later 'true' pyramids.

Abusir and Abu Ghurab

The four pyramids built in the Fifth Dynasty at Abusir were poorly made. The outer cladding was taken off and reused or made into lime.

The Pyramid of Sahura

Most of the reliefs that once decorated the temples of King Sahura have been lost. The few that survive show scenes from royal life. Sahura's successor, Neferirkara, planned a huge complex but it was never finished. The next king, Neuserra, used the causeway for his pyramid complex. King Raneferef built the fourth Abusir pyramid. The largest mastaba tomb belonged to the vizier Ptahshepses.

Sun Temples

Userkaf, founder of the Fifth Dynasty, built a huge temple to the sun god Ra. It looks like a pyramid complex because it has a causeway and a valley temple.

A well-preserved sun temple, dating from the reign of Neuserra, contains an open court with an altar and giant obelisk. The obelisk was a copy of a sacred stone in the temple of Ra at Heliopolis. The stone was a symbol of the first mound of land and the rays of the sun.

Pyramids at Giza

On the edge of modern Cairo is the plateau of Giza. The largest of the Egyptian royal tombs were built here in the Fourth Dynasty.

The Great Pyramid

The Great Pyramid is the popular name for the pyramid of Khufu (Cheops). Built almost 4,500 years ago, it was 147 metres (482 ft) tall and covered an area of 2,341 square metres (2,800 sq. yd). There were five boat pits nearby, three subsidiary pyramids and many mastaba tombs.

The Second and Third Pyramids

The slightly smaller pyramid next to the Great Pyramid belonged to Khufu's son, King Khephren. The much smaller third pyramid was that of King Menkaura.

Near the valley temple of Khephren, a huge outcrop of limestone was carved into a sphinx 73 metres (240 ft) long. Built with the body of a lion and the head of a king, the Great Sphinx was worshipped as the sun god. Pilgrims left offerings of miniature sphinxes and lions.

A reconstruction of Sahura's pyramid complex at Abusir. A causeway joins the riverside valley temple to the courtyard of the mortuary temple. There is one subsidiary pyramid.

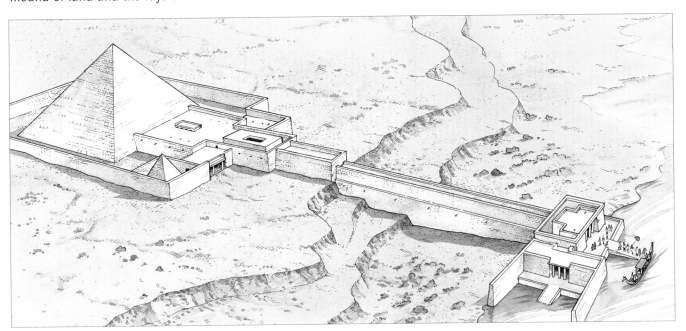

THE DELTA

The damp climate and marshy delta of Lower Egypt are not good for preserving ancient remains. The channels of the Nile have changed course, destroying towns. Stones from ancient temples and tombs were reused, and mud-bricks were turned into fertiliser. As a result, less is known about Lower Egypt than Upper Egypt.

Remains of Religious Sites

At Buto, the Delta goddess Wadjit was worshipped for three thousand years. The buried remains of a Predynastic settlement have produced pottery and building materials that show that the culture of Upper Egypt gradually overwhelmed the local culture.

Houses and tombs from the Old Kingdom have been found at the important religious sites of Bubastis and Tell el-Ruba (ancient Mendes). Archaeologists at Mendes have found a burned building full of bodies. This may be evidence of a civil war at the end of the Old Kingdom.

The Hyksos, foreign invaders, seized power in the delta in the Second Intermediate Period. They built the walled city of Avaris (modern Tell el-Daba). The early 18th Dynasty rulers who defeated the Hyksos erected a new palace at Avaris. It was decorated with wall paintings in the Cretan style.

Unrobbed Tombs

During the late New Kingdom, and for much of the Third Intermediate Period, the delta ruled Egypt. Many kings, princes and queens were buried inside temple enclosures in delta cities. Lots of treasures have been discovered in undisturbed royal tombs at Tanis and Tell el-Muqdam, and in the temple area at Bubastis.

Once the delta had temples that were as impressive as the temples that still stand today in southern Egypt. The temple of the goddess Neith at Sais was famous in the ancient world, but little remains today. Most of the great temple of Ra at Heliopolis was lost beneath the sprawling suburbs of modern Cairo.

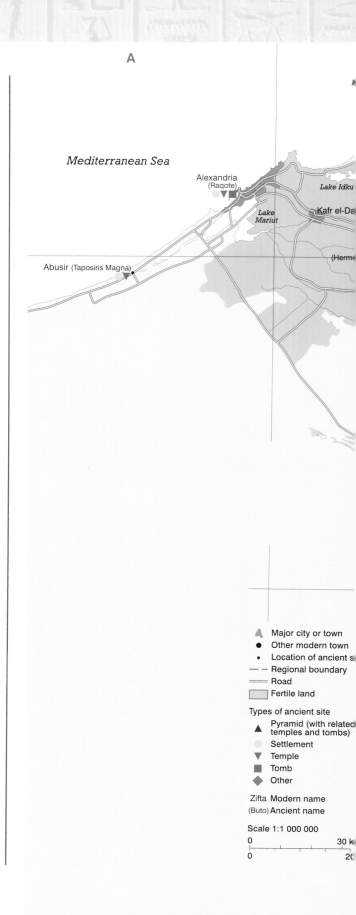

A

Mediterranean Sea

Alexandria (Raqote)

Lake Idku

Kafr el-Da

Lake Mariut

(Herme

Abusir (Taposiris Magna)

Major city or town
Other modern town
Location of ancient s
Regional boundary
Road
Fertile land

Types of ancient site
▲ Pyramid (with related temples and tombs)
Settlement
▼ Temple
■ Tomb
◆ Other

Zifta Modern name
(Buto) Ancient name

Scale 1:1 000 000
0   30 k
0   20

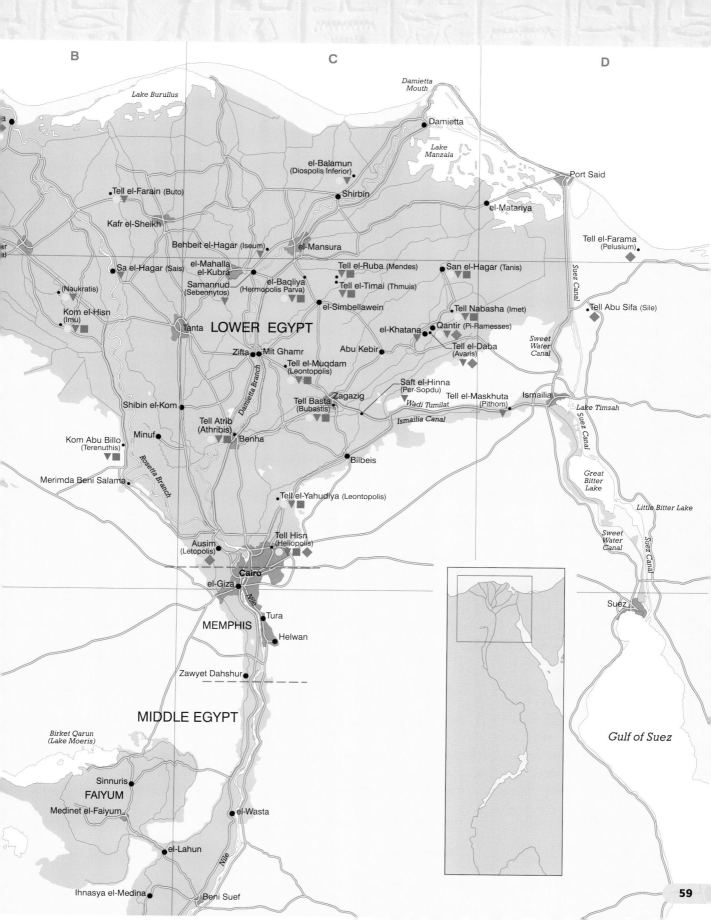

B

C

D

Lake Burullus

Damietta Mouth

Damietta

Lake Manzala

Port Said

el-Balamun
(Diospolis Inferior)

Shirbin

el-Mataria

Tell el-Farain (Buto)

Tell el-Farama
(Pelusium)

Kafr el-Sheikh

Behbeit el-Hagar (Iseum)

el-Mansura

Sa el-Hagar (Sais)

el-Mahalla
el-Kubra

Tell el-Ruba (Mendes)

San el-Hagar (Tanis)

(Naukratis)

Samannud
(Sebennytos)

el-Baqliya
(Hermopolis Parva)

Tell el-Timai (Thmuis)

Tell Abu Sifa (Sile)

Kom el-Hisn
(Imu)

el-Simbellawein

Tell Nabasha (Imet)

Tanta

LOWER EGYPT

el-Khatana

Qantir (Pi-Ramesses)

Sweet Water Canal

Zifta

Mit Ghamr

Abu Kebir

Tell el-Daba
(Avaris)

Tell el-Muqdam
(Leontopolis)

Saft el-Hinna
(Per-Sopdu)

Ismailia

Shibin el-Kom

Zagazig

Tell el-Maskhuta
(Pithom)

Lake Timsah

Tell Basta
(Bubastis)

Wadi Tumilat

Kom Abu Billo
(Terenuthis)

Minuf

Tell Atrib
(Athribis)

Benha

Ismailia Canal

Great Bitter Lake

Merimda Beni Salama

Bilbeis

Little Bitter Lake

Tell el-Yahudiya (Leontopolis)

Sweet Water Canal

Tell Hisn
(Heliopolis)

Ausim
(Letopolis)

Cairo

el-Giza

Suez

MEMPHIS

Tura

Helwan

Zawyet Dahshur

MIDDLE EGYPT

Gulf of Suez

*Birket Qarun
(Lake Moeris)*

Sinnuris

FAIYUM

Medinet el-Faiyum

el-Wasta

el-Lahun

Ihnasya el-Medina

Beni Suef

Nile

Damietta Branch

Rosetta Branch

Suez Canal

Bubastis

From the Old Kingdom onwards, Bubastis was an important town. It stood in an important strategic location where it controlled the trade routes from Memphis to the Sinai peninsula and farther east to Asia. The town was also the main cult centre for Bastet, the lioness goddess. It reached its greatest influence during the 22nd Dynasty. The kings of the dynasty came from Bubastis, where they erected beautiful buildings in honour of the goddess. The main temple to Bastet was rebuilt many times. During the Late Period the town was the capital of one of the nomes of Lower Egypt. It entered a decline in the first centuries CE.

Worshipping Bastet

The annual festival of Bastet was one of the most popular in all of Egypt. People travelled from all over Egypt to sing, dance and feast in honour of the cat goddess. One Greek writer said: "More wine is drunk at this festival than in the whole of the rest of the year" (Herodotus, *History* II). Herodotus also described the main temple dedicated to the goddess. In the middle of the fifth century BCE, when he wrote, the temple stood on a far lower level than the surrounding city. It stood on an island created from two arms of a sacred lake. Although archaeologists working at the temple confirm that Herodotus's description was accurate, they have been unable to determine the size of the building – it was anything from 200 to 300 metres (650 to 980 ft) long.

Cat Cemetery

Starting in the Third Intermediate Period, sacred cats were bred in the temple. They were buried in a special cat cemetery to the north of the town. Although the exact number of cats buried in the cemetery is unknown it is thought to run into millions. During the 19th century, thousands of cat mummies from Bubastis were shipped to Europe. Their remains were ground up and used as fertiliser.

Alexandria

Alexandria was the capital of the Ptolemies, the Greek dynasty that ruled Egypt from 332 to 30 BCE. It was founded by Alexander the Great and became a lively international centre. Its culture owed more to Greece and the Mediterranean than to Egypt. Although many Egyptians lived in the city, it was governed by Greeks. There was also a large and influential Jewish community. The city was the most important port in the Hellenistic world, and it played a key role in the spread of information about ancient Egypt during the Classical age.

Ancient Wonder

A tall lighthouse that stood on the island of Pharos in the busy harbour was considered to be one of the Seven Wonders of the Ancient World. It was topped by a huge flame that never went out. Alexandria had other important buildings, including the tomb of the city's founder, Alexander the Great, and a library that contained the largest collection of books in the ancient world. Under the Romans, villas, a sports stadium and public bath-houses were also built.

Archaeologists have discovered underground tombs close to the temple of the Greco–Egyptian god Serapis. The tombs show Greek style paintings of scenes from Egyptian religion. The Greeks borrowed some ideas from the Egyptians. Statues and other objects from older Egyptian buildings were brought to Alexandria to decorate the city, including a pair of obelisks from Heliopolis. One of the most famous remains is a stone column that is known as 'Pompey's pillar'. Like other ruins at Alexandria, it dates from the Roman period. However, the city was also home to many pieces of ancient Egypt statuary, such as sphinxes.

Parts of the ancient city have disappeared under the modern city. Earthquakes and gradual coastal erosion have destroyed other parts. Marine archaeologists are still excavating the harbour seabed, where they have already found many Egyptian and Hellenistic statues.

Tanis

The most impressive ruins of the whole delta region are found at Tanis. It was the capital of Egypt for much of the Third Intermediate Period. A great temple of Amon, founded by King Psusennes I, lies inside a double mud-brick enclosure wall. The temple was added to by successive Third Intermediate Period kings.

Remains from much earlier periods, such as stone blocks, columns, obelisks and statues, have been found at Tanis. They were taken from older buildings at other sites and were brought to Tanis to give it instant authority and splendour as the new capital.

A Golden Discovery

In 1939, a French archaeologist called Pierre Montet discovered underground tombs near the south-west corner of the temple. The tombs of four Intermediate Period kings lay there, and some of the burials were intact. Funeral objects included spectacular gold and silver jewellery as well as gold and silver vessels, including drinking cups. King Psusennes I was buried in a solid silver coffin and had a gold mummy mask.

Qantir

At two points the Qantir area was very important in Egyptian history. In the Second Intermediate Period, it was the site of Avaris, the capital of the Hyksos kings. Avaris was probably located in the south part of the Qantir district, close to present-day Tell el-Daba. The Theban king Ahmose took the city and partially destroyed it around 1540 BCE.

The Ramessid family came from this part of the delta. Ramesses II built a new city called Pi-Ramesses close to modern Qantir. In its day, it was one of the largest and most splendid cities of ancient Egypt. The palace area covered almost 9 hectares (22 acres) or the equivalent of nine soccer fields.

Today, almost nothing remains. Many of the major buildings were later taken apart to provide stone and statues for Tanis. It may have been the use of forced labour on the building of Pi-Ramesses that led to the Exodus of the Jews from Egypt.

The many channels and islands have long made the delta Egypt's most fertile area. Agricultural production supported the rise of numerous local dynasties, some of which ruled over all of Egypt.

GLOSSARY

Book of the Dead Spells written on papyrus and placed in tombs from the New Kingdom to the Greco-Roman Period. No single copy contains all 192 spells.

canopic jars Set of four jars to hold the vital organs removed from a mummy. The organs were the liver, lungs, stomach and intestines.

cartouche A sign representing an oval knot of rope. From the Fourth Dynasty, the king's two most important names were written inside cartouches. Cartouches were used on the king's documents and made into reliefs on the king's buildings and statues as a kind of seal.

Cataracts Stretches of dangerous rapids in the River Nile. There were six Cataracts between Aswan and Khartoum in Sudan.

colonnade A double row of columns roofed to form a passage, or a single row of columns joined by a roof to a wall.

cuneiform The Mesopotamian script, written on clay tablets with wedge-shaped strokes. Cuneiform tablets were found at el-Amarna.

deity A god or goddess. Egyptian deities can have human, semihuman or animal shapes.

demotic An Egyptian script for everyday use, developed in the seventh century BCE. It is one of the three scripts on the Rosetta Stone.

dynasty A series of rulers, usually related to each other by blood or marriage. The order of the Egyptian dynasties is known from the third-century BCE historian Manetho and from ancient lists of kings.

figurine A small statue of a god or goddess, a person or an animal. Figurines could be made of stone, wood, metal, faience or pottery.

hieroglyph A sign in the oldest Egyptian script. Most hieroglyphic signs are pictures of people, animals, plants or things. The word is Greek and means 'sacred carving'.

inundation The annual flooding of the River Nile between July and October. A 'good Nile' was a flood that covered all the agricultural land, leaving behind a fertile layer of mud. If the flood was too high, it swept away houses.

If the flood was too low, it would not cover all the fields. These were 'bad Niles'.

ka The spirit or 'double' of a living person. After death the ka needed offerings to survive. A dead person also had a ba (soul), shown as a human-headed bird.

mastaba A type of Early Dynastic and Old Kingdom tomb with a flat-roofed rectangular superstructure. The name comes from the Arabic word for a bench.

mummification The artificial preservation of bodies. Drying out the body was usually the most important part of the process.

natron A natural mixture of carbonate, bicarbonate, chloride and sodium sulphate. It was used in mummification and was an ingredient of faience.

necropolis A Greek term meaning 'city of the dead'. It refers to large and important burial areas, mainly on the edge of the desert.

nome Greek word for an administrative province of Egypt. The governor of a nome was a nomarch.

obelisk A tapering stone shaft with a tip shaped like a pyramid; a symbol of the sun's rays. Pairs of obelisks were often set up outside temples.

oracle A shrine where a god or goddess answered questions from worshippers, or a sign that was given by a deity in answer to a question.

papyrus A marsh plant (*Cyperus papyrus*) and a type of paper made from it. Also a scroll made from sheets of papyrus gummed together.

pharaoh A title for the king of Egypt from the late 18th Dynasty onwards. It means 'The Great House'—the Palace.

pylon The grand entrance to a temple, consisting of towers flanking a doorway.

pyramid A tomb in the shape of a geometric pyramid. This shape may have symbolised a stairway to heaven, the sun's rays or the first mound of land.

relief A scene carved in stone or wood.

sacred bark A special boat used by a statue of a deity on river journeys. Statues were often carried in model boats known as bark shrines.

sarcophagus Used in this book to mean the stone chest inside which a coffin was placed. A sarcophagus was rectangular or anthropoid (human body-shaped).

scarab A carving in the form of a scarab beetle (dung beetle). It represented Khepri, god of the rising sun. This 'sun beetle' was a very popular amulet shape. Scarabs were often inscribed with royal names.

scribe A person trained to read and write. Most scribes worked for the government.

shabti (or ushabti) Small figurines, usually in the shape of a mummy, placed in burials. Their magical purpose was to carry out any work the dead person might be told to do in the afterlife.

sphinx An Egyptian sphinx usually had the body of a lion and the head of a king or queen. It was a symbol of royal power and a form of the sun god.

stela A slab of stone or wood, usually with carved and painted texts and scenes. Stelae were set up in the outer areas of tombs and in temples a little like gravestones or commemorative plaques.

uraeus A symbol of kingship in the shape of a rearing cobra.

vizier The highest official in the Egyptian government. There were sometimes two viziers, one based at Memphis, the other at Thebes.

FURTHER RESOURCES

PUBLICATIONS

Ardagh, P. *The Hieroglyphs Handbook* (Scholastic, 2001).

Clare, J. D. *Pyramids of Ancient Egypt* (Harcourt Brace Jovanich, 1992).

Cohen, D. *Ancient Egypt* (Doubleday, 1990).

Galford, E. *Hatshepsut: The Princess Who Became King* (National Geographic, 2005).

Harris, G. *Gods and Pharaohs from Egyptian Mythology* (Shocken, 1983).

Harris, G., and D. Pemberton. *The British Museum Illustrated Encyclopaedia of Ancient Egypt* (NTC, 2000).

Hart, George. Ancient Egypt: Eyewitness Books. (Dorling Kindersley, 2008).

Hawass, Z. *Tutankhamun: The Mystery of the Boy King* (National Geographic, 2005).

Ikram, S. *Egyptology* (Amideast, 1997).

Millard, A. *Going to War in Ancient Egypt* (Franklin Watts, 2001).

Pemberton, D. *Egyptian Mummies: People from the Past* (Harcourt, 2000).

Rubalcaba, Jill. *Ancient Egypt: National Geographic Investigates.* (National Geographic Society, 2007)

Tiano, O. *Rameses II and Egypt* (Henry Holt & Co., 1996).

Reference books for adults

Baines, J., and J. Malek. *Cultural Atlas of Ancient Egypt* (Checkmark Books, 2000).

Ikram, S., and A. Dodson. *The Mummy in Ancient Egypt* (W. W. Norton & Co., 1998).

Lehner, M. *The Complete Pyramids* (W. W. Norton & Co., 1997).

Pinch, G. *Handbook of Egyptian Mythology* (ABC–Clio, 2002).

Redford, D. (ed.). *The Oxford Encyclopaedia of Ancient Egypt* (Oxford University Press, 2001).

Shaw, Ian. *The Oxford History of Ancient Egypt* (Oxford University Press, 2004).

Taylor, J. H. *Death and the Afterlife in Ancient Egypt* (University of Chicago Press, 2001).

WEB SITES

http://www.ancientegypt.co.uk
Pages about Egypt on the Web site of the British Museum, London.

www.ashmol.ox.ac.uk/Griffith.html
The Griffith Institute of Oxford, England, includes links for young people.

http://www.carlos.emory.edu/ODYSSEY
An interactive journey through ancient Egypt.

http://www.oi.uchicago.edu/OI/MUS/ED
The Oriental Institute of the University of Chicago education program.

http://www.guardians.net/egypt/kids
Fun and interesting Egypt links especially for children.

http://www.historyforkids.org
Community service learning project from Portland State University. Click on link to Egypt.

http://www.horus.ics.org.eg
Egyptian Web site designed and developed specially for kids around the world.

http://www.metmuseum.org/explore
The Metropolitan Museum of Art 'Explore and Learn' pages with links to ancient Egyptian art.

INDEX